C. A. Slaugh

Catlettsburg- Ky.

Septr 20. 1912

THE BUILDING OF THE CHURCH

BOOKS BY

CHARLES E. JEFFERSON, D.D., LL.D.

THINGS FUNDAMENTAL
THE CHARACTER OF JESUS
DOCTRINE AND DEED
THE NEW CRUSADE
MY FATHER'S BUSINESS
THE MINISTER AS PROPHET
QUIET HINTS TO GROWING PREACHERS
QUIET TALKS TO EARNEST PEOPLE
TALKS ON HIGH THEMES
THE BUILDING OF THE CHURCH

THE BUILDING OF THE CHURCH

CHARLES E. JEFFERSON

PASTOR OF THE BROADWAY TABERNACLE
NEW YORK CITY

New York
THE MACMILLAN COMPANY
1911

Copyright, 1910,

By THE MACMILLAN COMPANY.

———

Set up and electrotyped.   Published September, 1910.   Reprinted
November, 1910 ; April, November, 1911.

Norwood Press
J. S. Cushing Co. — Berwick & Smith Co.
Norwood, Mass., U.S.A.

THE lectures of this volume were delivered before the Divinity School of Yale University, in the months of April and May, 1910, on the Lyman Beecher Foundation.

CONTENTS

LECTURE I

THE CHURCH BUILDING IDEA
IN THE NEW TESTAMENT

THE CHURCH BUILDING IDEA IN THE NEW TESTAMENT

The sovereign interest which this lectureship holds in its eye — the work of Preaching — has not been overlooked in the choosing of my subject. I do not forget that I am speaking to men who are interested supremely in the art of preaching, but I invite you to approach the subject through the Christian church. After so many illustrious teachers have spoken on the subject, it would be indeed presumptuous for any man at this late date to attempt to offer additional suggestion or instruction, were it not that the subject of preaching lies, like the New Jerusalem, foursquare, with an ideal number of gates on every side, through any one of which the lecturer may make his way into the heart of the imperial theme. The traditional method of approach has been through the pulpit, an institution established for the proclamation of the Christian message; and when this method is adopted it is natural that the topic uppermost in the discussion should be either the message, its subject matter and its manner of treatment, or the messenger, his personality and character, his pulpit elocution and gestures, his literary habit and style. This method of approach is the direct and obvious one, and is not without great rewards. Like all methods, however, it has its limitations, and carries with it certain perils which, unless guarded against, are likely to work mischief. It is easily possible to think of the work of preaching too narrowly, to imagine that it is a matter concerning supremely one individual — the man in the pulpit. One may come under the sway of the idea that in any discussion of the work of preaching the preacher himself is the primary, if not the sole, object of study, that it is upon his mental endowments and spiritual attainments that the success of the sermon chiefly depends, and that in the education of ministers attention ought to be jealously focussed on those disciplines by which the preacher is most surely fitted to deliver acceptably a pulpit discourse.

But preaching, when we look at it long enough, is seen to involve, not one man only, but a society of men. No preacher lives to himself nor dies to himself. He is an organ functioning in an organism, finding his life in the vital relations by which he is bound to other lives. His endowments and attainments are only one factor in the work of preaching, another factor of no less importance being the attainments and endowments of the Christian society. The sermon is not the voice of an isolated individual, but the utterance of a body of men baptized into the name of Jesus. The sermon comes not out of the preacher alone, but out of the church. The preacher gives back what he receives. He cannot feed himself. He is nourished by his environment — the family of Christ. He cannot shape himself. He is moulded by the body of believers. He cannot grow in isolation. He is a plant dependent on the atmosphere and the weather, both of which are largely the creation of the Christian people. The church cannot wisely be ignored in any comprehensive study of the preacher's work, nor can it be shoved into the background without loss. The traditional method has been to reach the church through the preacher. Let us in this course of lectures try to reach the preacher through the church. It has become the fashion to come to the congregation through the sermon. It may prove advantageous to come to the sermon through the congregation. The church is older than the pulpit, the congregation antedates the preacher. It was not the pulpit which created the church, but the church which created the pulpit. It is not the preacher who keeps alive the Christian society; it is the Christian society which keeps alive the preacher.

In an earnest study, therefore, of preaching, we are justified in beginning with the church, the spiritual society through which the preacher first came to be, and by which preaching is ever nourished and kept vital.

There are special reasons why this method of approach is just now not only opportune, but likely to prove most rewarding, one of which is that the church is in many quarters thrown into the shadow. Owing to the multiplication of organizations engaged in ethical and philanthropic work, the church does not loom so large in the public eye as formerly. Surrounded by a host of religious and semireligious bodies, it is partially hidden by them, and its glory once unique and splendidly impressive, is somewhat shorn. Moreover, there is a new world view point, and everything has come to judgment. All the fundamental institutions of humanity — the family, the state, the church — have been thrown into the crucible and are being tried by fire. There are voices declaring that the family as hitherto existing is a fountain flowing plagues and curses, to be superseded by something better ; and that the state, as the world has thus far known it, is an instrument of injustice and oppression, to be thrown upon the scrap heap of worn-out institutions. In an age so radical, it is not to be wondered at that the church of Christ should be scrutinized with hostile eyes and classed by many among those curious organisms which have a trick of surviving their usefulness. There is a great company of thoughtful people for whom the Christian church has no significance. Some of them ignore it altogether, others notice it only to smile at it as a survival of a waning superstition, or to curse it as an obstacle to progress. To others it had a place; but to-day, alas, its creeds are all out-grown, its methods antiquated, its power is dwin-dling, and the wisdom of perpetuating it in its present form is questionable. The seat of the scornful is crowded, and so also is the seat of the mournful, the seat wherein congregate the good people who are always lamenting the decay of the pulpit and the decline of the church. When they look backward, they see pulpit giants; when they look round them, they see pulpit dwarfs. The church was mighty once, but not now. These are the people who write newspaper articles on "the decadence of the pulpit," who publish novels showing that if Christlike people desire to ac-complish anything worth while, they must cut loose from the church, who deliver lectures in which the most sparkling paragraphs are gibes at the preachers and thrusts at the church members. The most vigorous and plausible criticism of our day is directed, not against the person of Jesus nor his ethical teaching, but against the institution which bears his name. It is a good time for all who intend to preach to think about the church.

Many preachers are thinking little about it, and others are thinking about it mistakenly. The very word "church" is in many pulpits tabooed. There are clergymen who preach no longer about the church. Their favorite theme is the "Kingdom of God." An influential American theologian, in a valuable treatise on theology, picks up the word "church" only to drop it, using in its place "The Christian People." An English preacher, whose praise is in all the churches, and who although dead yet speaks, keeps saying in one of his most popular volumes that it is to be regretted that Paul did not say less about the church and more about the Kingdom, because the characteristic product of the church is ecclesiastics, whereas the characteristic product of the Kingdom is philanthropists. An eminent German theologian has informed us that the church is not an essential part of the religion of Jesus. Christianity needs, he says, no dogma, no organization, and no ritual. Christianity, when rightly understood, is simply a filial disposition in the heart. When those who sit in the seats of the mighty speak after this fashion, it is not to be wondered at that men lower down begin to think of the church with a slackened reverence and to speak of it with a diminished enthusiasm. The church has to many Christians become an object to be apologized for, and has ceased to be an institution to be sacrificed for and loved. There is no doctrine of the Christian creed in which it is so easy for young men to-day to go astray as the doctrine of the Christian church.

The effect of this widespread scepticism in regard to the church is manifesting itself increasingly. The diminished attendance at theological seminaries on both sides of the sea is a subject of troubled discussion, and many an explanation has been offered. It is singular that one of the root causes has been generally overlooked altogether. Young men in diminished numbers are preparing themselves for the ministry, largely because the impression is abroad that the pulpit is in a state of decay, that ministers are no longer men of influence, that the church is obsolescent, and that there are other and better ways in which a Christian man can

make his life count in the work of social betterment.
Our age is not a whit more materialistic than all
other ages have been. The young men of our day
have as high ideals as young men have ever had,
their impulses are as generous and noble, their
faith in Christ is as deep and secure, their ambition
to serve humanity has never been surpassed; but
never have men been so practical as now. They
want opportunity to do something worth while, they
desire to make their lives count for the utmost
possible, and many of them hesitate to enter the
ministry, because they have heard it said by
Christian men — it may be by a Christian college
president, or a Christian college professor, or a
Christian editor, or a Christian business man —
that the pulpit is a waning power, that it offers
opportunities for service far inferior to those
offered in other fields. Many a young man has
recently turned his back on the ministry because he
was unwilling to consecrate his life to the propping
up of an institution which, in the estimation of so
many Christian men in whose judgment he has
confidence, is anæmic and likely to collapse. It
is chiefly because the church of God as a divine
and mighty and indispensable institution has fallen
into disrepute, that we find ourselves facing the

question, "How can we increase the number of candidates for the ministry?"

It is sad to see a man turning away from the ministry because he does not understand the church, but it is tragic to see one entering the ministry with a wrong attitude to the church. Young ministers sometimes look upon the church as a necessary evil, an inherited encumbrance, a sort of device by which preachers are handicapped in their movements and held back from largest usefulness. Men of this type are eager to get at what they call the world. Their desire is to reconstruct the social order. They want to do things on a broad scale. To deal with so small and insignificant a body as a church seems parochial and belittling. All they want is a pulpit, a place in which to stand and thunder forth their message. They eye church officials with suspicion. They would rather work alone. They are sorry they must stay in a church building. A theatre would suit them better. As for pastoral visitation, they abhor it. It eats up time which ought to be given to the proclamation of ideas and the correction of evils. To be sure, a church has its uses. It can furnish the minister's salary and pay the sexton, but, outside of this, its usefulness is problematic.

Ordinarily it is in the way, and time spent upon it might better be otherwise employed. When a minister of this stripe goes into a parish the first man he visits is the printer. He believes in printer's ink. Printer's ink will let the people know he is there. He does not know that a living church is better for advertising purposes than all the printing presses in the town. He scatters cards to reach the masses. He has yet to learn that the preacher best reaches the masses who knows best how to reach his church. He is furious to get at the crowd, and in order to get at it he is willing to trample on his church. It is as if a school-teacher in order to educate a community should turn his back on his school, or a physician in order to heal the town should ignore his hospital, or that a general in haste to annihilate the enemy should do away with his army. He burns to reconstruct the world, not suspecting that the particular section of the world which first needs reconstruction at his hands is his own church. He is burdened with the conviction that he is ordained to fight the world, the flesh, and the devil, and in his innocence he does not know that all these are waiting for him in his church.

If it is a blunder to ignore the church in an effort

to reach the masses, it is a more serious blunder to slight the church in one's direct dealings with it. Some ministers take hold of a church as though it were a lump of putty or a piece of wood to be shaped at their will. They do not give it credit for having a soul of its own. They begin at once to reorganize it. They set out before breakfast to make it all over. Nothing about it suits them. The Sunday-school is on a wrong basis. The young people's society has faulty methods. The Woman's Missionary Circle has an antiquated constitution. Even the Cradle Roll must have a new set of by-laws. All these changes must be made immediately. The new minister does not know that the church has a disposition and temperament of its own, that its personality is as distinct and solid as his, that it is an organism with traditions which are sacred and customs which are hallowed, with notions and whims that must be respected, and with idiosyncrasies which cannot safely be ignored. Blessed is the preacher who realizes that he is only a sojourner as all his fathers were. He stands in the line of a long succession. Other men have labored and he is entering into their labors. It is not for him to start out as though the world were just beginning. The church was there before he was born. It will be there after he is dead. He is not a clerical Robinson Crusoe on a desert island. The shore is covered with human tracks. If he is a man of sense he will take note of them, and observe the direction in which men have been moving. The first thing in the town for a preacher to take notice of is his church. Let him begin at once to study it, to strive to understand it, to come into sympathy with it, to plan for it, to render himself useful to it, to make himself a part of it, and in this way he will come to love it. When he once loves it, he will possess the first requisite of a successful preacher.

If it is hazardous to slight the church in the work of administration, it is fatal to ignore it in the work of preaching. Young ministers are often rich in note-books when they go into their first parish, and they begin to work out of their note-books toward the church. This is a blunder and often leads the saints to say sundry uncomplimentary things about theological seminaries. Preachers should work from their parish toward their note-books. It is the church which must determine the character of the pulpit instruction and the sequence of it. The church is a growing organism and the preacher must know the stage of its development before he can feed it. He cannot use the material in his note-books before he finds out whether that is the material which is just now needed. Possibly the contents of his notes may be wet sawdust, possibly gunpowder. They may dampen and deaden, or they may cause an explosion. Men sometimes are blown out of their pulpit by working from their note-books toward the church, instead of from the church toward their note-books. Let a man find out what the church is able to digest and assimilate, and then go to his books in search of it. A physician always looks at his patient before he goes to the medicine chest. A wise preacher begins, not with his books, but with his church.

The old question of ministerial liberty is always coming up to torment us, and the scandals caused by preachers insisting on what they call their rights are among the most vexing with which the church has to deal. Every Christian minister is of course free, but freedom has its laws. Liberty is precious, but it has its limitations. Because a minister is free it does not follow that he has a right to proclaim from the pulpit everything he reads or everything which he happens to be thinking. Certain men are always getting confused at this point. Their bewilderment is due to a forgetting of the church.

A man comes to think of himself as being the church. He forgets that the faith was delivered to the saints — the entire body of the Lord's followers. He is only one man among many. A theological education does not give him the right to set himself in a class apart, and to count himself independent of the Christian brotherhood. He is not a pulpit pope. He has his rights, but so also have other Christians. He wishes to be free, so also do his brethren. There is a liberty of hearing as well as a liberty of speaking. In asserting what he calls his freedom, he may rob others of the liberties which belong to them as Christian men. The church of Christ stands in the world as the ordained teacher of definite conceptions of God and man, of duty and destiny, of Jesus of Nazareth and the Holy Spirit, of the church and the sacraments; and if a preacher in the course of his mental evolution comes to reject any of the beliefs which the church counts fundamental, there is nothing for him to do but to retire. To promise to teach a certain set of beliefs and then proceed to repudiate them, is not exercising the liberty of prophesying, but simply failing to keep one's word. One is always at liberty to withdraw from the Christian pulpit as soon as he has surrendered the Christian creed.   The man who wants to know what are his liberties as a teacher must work, not from himself toward the church, but from the church toward himself.

Sometimes it is not so much a question of preaching fundamental doctrine as of proclaiming certain ethical principles, and attacking certain undoubted moral evils.   Here again the preacher must begin by establishing right relations between himself and his church.   It is often said that under our American plan of ministerial support, a preacher is constantly tempted to hold back unpalatable teaching, and is in danger of degenerating into a flatterer or demagogue.   The danger is real, but can easily be escaped.   If a man has a contemptuous view of his church he is well-nigh certain to be afraid of it. But love casts out fear.   If a man loves his church and proves his love by his life, he can say to it anything which is proper for a Christian teacher to say to his pupils, anything which it is fitting for a Christian man to say to his friends.   The preachers who get into trouble by talking plainly to their people are as a rule preachers who do not love their churches.   If a man stays in his study through the week, wishing he could get a call to a larger church, secretly despising the flock of which he is the ap-

c

pointed shepherd, and then goes into the pulpit on the Lord's day, and thunders against his people's sins, there may be a storm, and there ought to be. No man has a right to chide or condemn men, unless he has won the right by loving them. It is a clear vision of the church which preachers most need when they come to deal with questions of liberty in the proclamation of their message.

Another outstanding phenomenon of our age is the shortening of pastorates. This is due in part to hazy conceptions of the preacher's supreme work. If a man thinks his mission in the world is the delivering of sermons, he is likely to want to pass from parish to parish, staying only long enough in each pulpit to exhaust his sermonic stock. Such a man is a sermonizer, but not a church builder. He has been trained to write sermons, but not instructed in the art of church building. He does not know what the supreme work of a minister of Christ is. He does not know what preaching is for. His knowledge does not run beyond the A B C's of his calling. He thinks of himself as a man whose sole business is to convert sinners. Having persuaded sinners to say they want to follow Christ, and having induced them to unite with the church, his labor, he thinks, is ended. It does not occur to him that the most difficult part of the minister's work is with people after they have joined the church. The minister is a teacher, and a teacher's real work begins only after the pupils are enrolled. He is the general of an army, and a general's critical task is drilling his men after they have enlisted, and massing them in such ways as to conquer the foe. He is a master-builder, and his task is not simply collecting material, but shaping it into a structure which shall become a shrine of the Eternal. The crowning and crucial work of a minister is not conversion, but church building. A man who does nothing but convert men is an evangelist, and should never be intrusted with a church. His work is of value, but is easily overestimated. He deserves a high place, but not the highest. The highest place belongs to the man who, year after year, in the same parish, instructs men in the high and difficult art of living together, and trains them by long and patient processes in the work of bringing spiritual forces to bear upon the moral problems of the community. The work of the evangelist is necessarily spectacular, and often bewitches the eyes of men who are young. Evangelism seems, sometimes, to young men a more Christlike and sacrificial form of service than the work performed in the course of the ordinary ministry; but the fact is that the work of the evangelist is not nearly so taxing either upon brain or heart as is the work performed by a man who through a long series of years gives himself devotedly to the soul-exhausting labor of knitting the lives of men together and building them up in righteousness. Young preachers in quiet and obscure parishes, reading of the exploits of famous evangelists moving in triumphal procession across the land, sometimes grow discontented, and wish that they too might leap upon a larger stage and play a thrilling part in the great drama of world redemption. But it should not be forgotten that it is not simply the men who scatter seed, but the men also who cultivate the grain and garner the harvest who win the right to a place among the world's benefactors. Converting men only once amounts ordinarily to little. They must be converted many times. Faces must be turned in the right direction, but what avails this, unless hesitant and stumbling feet are trained to walk toward the goal. The preacher who induces men to turn to God and join the church does well, but his supreme work as a Christian preacher is building converts into a brotherhood. The young preacher who at the end of the second year in a parish says, "My work is done," does not know what he is saying. It may be that his stock of star sermons is exhausted, or that the available outside sinners have all handed in their names; but if he understood a minister's mission, he would see that his work has scarcely begun. In two years a man can learn something of the nature of the material with which he has to deal, but the critical and arduous work of building lies still ahead of him. No matter how long he stays, there will be more work to do than there was in sight at the beginning. Men who engage in the building of the church know that the work is never done.

One cannot help wondering if not a little of the restlessness and discontent which fill the hearts of so many pastors is not due to confused notions of their relation to the church. Many a preacher has a hungry heart because he has never yet gotten close enough to his people. Preaching is a lonely business. A man sweats blood in preaching, and oftentimes the nerves are left unstrung. How can a preacher do his work except in an atmosphere made warm by Christian affection? In the earlier years it is exhilarating to preach, because one finds relief in self-expression. But as the years go on, there is less delight in the mere act of saying things, and the heart craves more and more the fellowship of kindred minds. A preacher who does not love his church, and whom his church does not love, is of all men most pitiable. Many a minister's career would have been a different one, had he only come to his pulpit by way of his church.

Turning now from the voices of an age which has become confused in its idea of the church, let us open the scriptures and purge our eyes by gazing upon the church as the writers of the New Testament saw it. With whom may we more fittingly begin than with that preacher without a peer — St. Paul? In genius and consecration, in passion and power, no ambassador of Christ in the long roll of the Christian centuries has written his name above the name of the man of Tarsus. Like many a modern critic, Paul at one time looked upon the church contemptuously. The prophet of Nazareth, having run his short and ignominious career, had vanished, leaving behind him a company of fanatics to be resisted and if possible annihilated. The fiery disciple of Gamaliel breathed forth threatenings and slaughter against this novel and accursed form of heresy. But one day, when his hand was uplifted ready to strike the little church in Damascus, Paul heard Jesus saying,

"Why persecutest thou me?" In this question there came a twofold revelation — a revelation of the character of Jesus, and a revelation of the relation of Jesus to his church. To his amazement Paul discovered that Jesus is not only living, but that he is identified with his church, and that it is impossible to slight, despise, or oppose the church without wounding the Son of God himself. From that hour to his death Paul knew but two sovereign themes — one was Jesus Christ, the other was the church. The only sin whose memory burned like fire in his heart was the sin which he had committed against the church. When you find him with his face in the dust, it is his persecution of the church which he is bewailing. When he declares he is the chief of sinners and that he is not worthy to be called an apostle, it is because the recollection of his sin against the church rolls over him like a flood. When you seek him at his highest, jubilant and enraptured, you find him thinking of the church. It is a subject never absent from his mind. He ransacks his vocabulary in search of figures by which adequately to image forth his idea of the church's character and mission. Sometimes he thinks of it as the household of faith — the family of Jehovah. At other times he sees it as the temple of God, the

very seat and shrine of the Eternal. Again it
presents itself to him as the body of Christ, the organism in which Christ's spirit operates, the instrument by which the soul of Christ works. Still again
it rises before him beautiful and radiant as a woman
in the hour of her greatest loveliness, the bride
of the world's Redeemer. Now and again he sees
it lifting itself superbly as the pillar and ground of
the truth, holding aloft in the eyes of the nations
the mystery of godliness — Jesus. Always it is
to him the medium of revelation, the organ through
which the Almighty speaks both to men and to
angels. "And now unto me, who am less than the
least of all saints, was this grace given, to preach
unto the Gentiles the unsearchable riches of Christ,
to the intent that now unto the principalities and the
powers in the heavenly places might be made known
through the church the manifold wisdom of God."
It was when he wrote to his maturest converts —
those in Corinth and Ephesus — that he had most
to say about the church. The theme of the pro-
foundest of all his letters — that to the Ephesians
— is the church of Christ. To regret that Paul has
so much to say about the church is to repine that
Christianity is not other than it is.

Paul's favorite figure of the church is a temple,

and he loved to think of himself as a master-builder. Jesus Christ is the foundation stone and Christian ministers all build on him.   Christian believers are little temples to be carefully built into the walls of a vast temple.   "Know ye not that ye are a temple of God, and that the spirit of God dwelleth in you ? If any man destroyeth the temple of God, him shall God destroy ; for the temple of God is holy, which temple ye are."   It is interesting to note how this figure haunts the Apostle, shaping and coloring his language, and cropping out in unexpected ways and places.   For the temples built of gold and silver and precious stones, Paul substituted the temple to be built of immortal souls; and to work for the en- largement and adorning of this temple was to him the greatest privilege which the good God can bestow. It was the vision of this temple with which he strove to inflame the hearts of his converts, and by means of which he braced his own intrepid spirit when the sky was full of thunder.   "Ye are no more stran- gers," he cries, "and sojourners, but ye are fellow citizens with the saints, and of the household of God, being built upon the foundation of the apostles and prophets, Christ Jesus himself being the chief corner-stone, in whom each several building, fitly framed together, groweth into a holy temple in the

Lord; in whom ye also are builded together for a habitation of God in the Spirit." This then is the work which the God and Father of Jesus Christ wishes to accomplish, and his plan is to do it by the coöperation of Christian men. Paul considered not only himself, but all church officials from the highest to the lowest as church builders. "And he gave some to be apostles; and some, prophets; and some, evangelists; and some, pastors and teachers, for the perfecting of the saints unto the work of ministering unto the building up of the body of Christ." The sentence has been marred for English readers by a faulty translation and a mistaken punctuation. It has been cut into three sections as though there were three separate and distinct things which Christian ministers are ordained to do. There is in fact only one thing. Their work is to equip or furnish believers for the work of ministering with a view to the building up of the body of Christ, which is Paul's name for the church. The building of the church is the supreme aim of every minister who holds Paul's view of the work of the Christian ministry.

The task of building belongs to all believers, and in order to train believers in the art of building, ministers of various ranks and endowments are selected and anointed by the supreme head of the church. It is because Paul always considers himself a builder that he employs so frequently the word which in Latin is "edify" but which in Anglo-Saxon is "build." His conception of himself as builder dictates to him the vocabulary of his sermons. "In the church I had rather speak five words with my understanding that I might instruct others also, than ten thousand words in a tongue." He will not use a tongue because it does not build up. How can men be built up by words whose meaning they do not know? If a man forgets that he is a church builder, he is well-nigh certain to employ a tongue, it may be scientific, or philosophical, or literary, or bookish, which while pleasing to himself is not intelligible to those to whom he preaches. If all Christian preachers since the days of Paul had only held fast Paul's conception of the aim of preaching as church building, not so many of them would have soared into the clouds of scintillating phrases, or plunged into the muddy depths of what they were pleased to call "thought." It is because Paul was a builder that he wrote sentences such as this, "If meat maketh my brother to stumble, I will eat no flesh forevermore." Why not? Because many lawful acts are not expedient. Actions that are lawful do not always build up. A Christian minister is not to do the thing which he has an abstract right to do, but the thing which will build up the church. The conception of church building then is the one by which a minister's conduct is to be largely controlled and directed. Whatever builds up the church is good for a minister to do, whatever pulls down the church a minister ought to avoid. The minister who stands on his legal rights while his church slowly disintegrates, or who pushes a pet policy even though he sees that it is splitting the church asunder, does not act on the principle by which the first great Christian preacher was guided. It is possible to be too insistent on one's rights, too conscious of one's deserts. A man with both eyes open to his rights is likely to be blind to the glory of the church. Knowledge of one's rights puffs up, love for the church builds up. Stubbornness and vanity often wear the garb of conscientiousness and consecration. When the question arises, "Which shall be sacrificed, the preacher or the church?" the man who follows Paul will be swift to give the right answer. The most pious of ministers may become one of the most dangerous and wicked of men if he writes himself large and the church

small.   Men who tear churches to pieces deserve
to be cast out with the publicans and heathen.

But laymen and preachers are bound by the
same principles.   Laymen as well as preachers are
church builders.   A good definition of a Christian
would be, "a builder of the church of Jesus Christ."
"Build one another up," so wrote the master builder
to a company of Christians in Thessalonica.   It is
an exhortation of perennial significance.   Men
become dilapidated as stone walls do.   The mortar
rots and the stones fall apart.   Human nature
crumbles and character goes to pieces.   The virtues
of the soul fall asunder and men need to be rebuilt.
This is the work which Christians must do for one
another, and it is a service in which the apostle
exhorts them to abound.   "Seek that ye may
abound in the work of building up."   "Let each
one of us please his neighbor for that which is good,
unto building up" — so he wrote to the members
of the church in Rome.   "Let us follow after things
which make for peace, and things whereby we may
build one another up" — this is the gist of what he
said to all the churches.   Many of the church
members of the first century had not grasped the
idea of building.   Religion to them was an individualistic possession, a treasure to be prized, an

experience to be enjoyed. They did not conceive of themselves as members of a society, organs of an organism, stones in a temple; and the result was frequent discord and distressing scandal. Men followed their own bent, indulged their vanity, gave vent to their censorious temper, pulled to pieces the unity of the congregation. In no church were conditions worse than in the church in Corinth. Considerateness and forbearance were virtues slightly practised, vanity and self-seeking were vices in full bloom. To this church the grieved apostle unfolds his idea of building. He shows how the abuses of public worship arise — Christians forget that they are builders. He feels that the sins which bring reproach on the name of Jesus would disappear if men gave themselves to the work of building. His counsel is summed up in the single sentence : "Let everything be done with a view to building."

This is a fit motto for a minister to inscribe above the desk on which he writes his sermons. The preacher is first of all a builder. He deals in affirmations, not in denials. He constructs, and only incidentally tears down. He is an architect and not an iconoclast. It is an evil spirit which takes delight in pulling things to pieces. Let a preacher beware of negations, especially during the first five years of his ministry. Youth has a fatal fondness for negations. Let the beginning preacher preach what he believes, and not tomahawk the doctrines which he has discarded. The preacher who brandishes an axe in the eyes of his congregation, hewing down with glee discredited dogmas and outgrown interpretations, need not be surprised if the church is shaken and his pulpit is rendered insecure. It is not courage, but lack of sense, which usually gets preachers into trouble. Laymen are as a rule not unwilling to listen to new conceptions which have a show of reasonableness; but the man who tears to pieces their old truth with a chuckle and stamps upon it with a whoop is sure to be resisted. It is not in human nature to relish reiterated and gloating declarations that nearly all one's old beliefs are both false and silly. If a man has really worked his way into broader and nobler conceptions, let him give his new vision in such a way that the church shall be lifted up and strengthened. Let every sentence of the sermon be written with a view, not to pulling down men who are dead, but to building up men who are alive. The words which might profitably be written across the preacher's study wall might wisely be inscribed in characters of gold before the eyes of all the congregation. What a transformation there will be in public worship, what a revolution in many a disciple's life, and what a reformation in the whole temper and conduct of many a Christian congregation, when once the idea is firmly grasped that all the followers of Jesus, both the man in the pulpit and the men in the pew, have for their heaven-appointed mission the building of the church !

Whence did Paul get his idea of church building ? Whence did it come to Peter ? To Peter also the church is the family of God, and his two exhortations stand side by side : "Love the brotherhood, Fear God." To Peter likewise the church is a living temple. To Peter, no less than to Paul, Jesus is the foundation stone, the stone rejected but chosen of God and precious, upon which living stone believers are built up a spiritual house. To Peter's eyes also the glory has vanished from temples made with hands, and now resides in the spiritual temple, the church of the living God. Whence came this passionate devotion to the church, and how did it happen that both apostles loved to think of it as a building ? The source of both the conception and the passion was undoubtedly the Son of God. It was at Cæsarea Philippi — so Matthew tells us

— at a critical moment in Jesus' life, when there occurred a twofold confession. The first was by Simon Peter, "Thou art the Christ, the Son of the Living God." This was the first full-toned recognition by man of the heavenly origin and character of Jesus. For this Jesus had been waiting. It is now time for him to make his confession. "Blessed art thou, Simon Bar-Jona: for flesh and blood hath not revealed it unto thee, but my father which is in heaven. And I also say unto thee, that thou art Peter, and upon this rock I will build my church: and the gates of Hades shall not prevail against it." There is an enthusiasm in these words which glows and flashes. They carry in their body the leaping joy of an exultant spirit. The declaration fell upon the air with the thrill of a new revelation. One feels that a secret long held back has leaped into the light. A man has at last recognized the presence of the world's Messiah, and to him and to his comrades who share his insight and conviction is now revealed what the Messiah has come to earth to do. It is his purpose to establish a society, a brotherhood, an institution which shall incorporate his spirit and perpetuate his work. The revelation was not given to the crowd. The crowd could not understand it or make use of it. The highest truths are

D

reserved for those who have ears to hear. The twelve did not at first grasp the full meaning of the words spoken at Cæsarea Philippi. They understood them better after the Day of Pentecost. They are words which even now are often imperfectly apprehended. They express a plan of God which can be only spiritually discerned.

Arguments are sometimes urged to prove that the church was a matter of indifference to Jesus. He cared only for ideas — men say — and the Christian church was an after-thought of his ambitious followers. As evidence for the soundness of this contention, it is said in triumph that Jesus never so much as mentioned the church but twice, consequently he cared nothing for it. It is indeed a wooden principle of interpretation, just now in vogue, which measures the importance of a fact by the number of times it is mentioned in the Scriptures. This is surrendering the use of intellect and settling difficult and spiritual questions by rule of thumb. It would seem then that he knows best the meaning of the New Testament who is quickest in the art of counting. But a thing may exist without the name, and a mere mathematician will never understand the gospels. Many things of moment Jesus never dealt with at all, because those lessons had been already learned. There are wide gaps in his recorded sayings because much was taken for granted by the men who wrote the gospels. That a religion could live and conquer without organization and without officials was an idea unthinkable to every first century Jew. Moreover there were subjects about which Jesus could not speak in public without hastening a crisis. One of such subjects was his Messiahship. He announced it so guardedly and so incidentally that certain New Testament scholars have declared that he never taught it at all. It was a fact to be spiritually apprehended and left to make its way in the world by the power of its own spirit. To have shouted it from the housetop would have forced forward the last act of the drama. What is true of his Messiahship is true also of his church. How could he have spoken of his church before the bigoted devotees of the Jewish church without precipitating the tragedy which it was necessary for a season to postpone? Things held in reserve are not therefore unimportant. It may be their tremendous importance which makes necessary the reticence concerning them. Jesus did not speak of the church in public for reasons perfectly clear, preferring to use terms which would excite least suspicion and create least irritation in the hearts he was trying to reach.   But while he made no public announcement, he pondered the church in his heart and gave himself unreservedly, from the day at Cæsarea Philippi onward, to the knitting of the souls of twelve men into a brotherhood, which should go on enlarging until it had embraced the world.   To a man whose eyes are not holden, the church is a towering and ubiquitous fact of the gospels.   In the upper chamber, on the last night, it is to his church that Jesus speaks.   To it and it only he gives the promise of the Holy Spirit; for it and it only he offers his high-priestly prayer; to it and it only he presents himself after his resurrection, and to it and only to it he gives the great commission.   "Go, disciple the nations."   Not to any individual believer, but to the society of believers, is the assurance granted of ultimate and unimaginable victory.

When it is said that Jesus did not found the church, language is used which needs explanation. If by founding the church is meant giving to a set of men a definite constitution and by-laws, with minute regulations as to polity and officials, then one may correctly say that Jesus did not found the church.   But when one considers his work upon the twelve, and what the one hundred and twenty did immediately after the Spirit — his Spirit — had come upon them, which Spirit he had expressly declared would lead them into truth, one is driven to the conclusion that it was Jesus who organized the Christian church, and that he and he alone can rightfully be called its Founder. If we are to accept the book of the Acts as authentic history, and are to believe in the guidance of the Holy Spirit, then we cannot escape the conclusion that the organization of the church was the act of Jesus, because the men who were the nearest to him in life and in death, and who were flooded with his spirit after a cloud had received him from their sight, threw themselves at once into the work of organizing believers into churches baptized into his name. The promise had been : "The Holy Spirit shall take the things of mine and show them un- to you," and the first thing shown to them was the Christian church. The church is the inevitable and indestructible creation of Christ's spirit. That he founded it and that it is the expression of his will, is also evidenced by Christian experience. His- tory proves that the continuance of Christianity is dependent upon the church. The church is an essential constituent of the Christian religion. The principles of Jesus do not enthrone themselves in human society without the assistance of the church. The church is in literal truth the body of Jesus. Without it he does no mighty deeds. The amount of work which he accomplishes in every country is conditioned on the character of the church in that country. The kind of service he performs in any community is determined by the character of the Christian society in that community. Whenever the church prospers, society improves. Whenever the church languishes, society degenerates. When the church is vigorous and spiritual, the social atmosphere becomes bracing and clear; when the church becomes worldly and corrupt, the sun is turned into darkness and the moon into blood. The principles of Jesus take root in pagan lands only when they are planted there and watered by the church. The gospel would never have gotten out of Palestine had it not been for the Christian brotherhood, nor out of Europe into England had it not been for the church, nor out of the Old World into the New had the church not sent it. There is no hope for the triumph of the Christian religion outside the church. Therefore, "I will build my church." It is his. He is the architect. Preachers in hours of despondency should listen to him saying : "I will build my church." "Unless the Lord build the house, they labor in vain who build it." He is at work. The church is no little private enterprise of ours. It is his. We are colaborers with him. He is ever by our side. The gates of death shall not prevail. Critics rage and brilliant writers imagine a vain thing. Kings and rulers in divers realms take counsel together and agree that the glory of the church is departing. He that sitteth in the heavens laughs. The Lord holds them in derision. The church is not obsolescent. Humanity has not outgrown it. Its noon is not behind it. Its triumphal career has only begun. We are toiling amid the mists of the early morning. It is the rising sun which smites our foreheads, and we cannot even dream of the glory which is to be. We work upon an enduring institution. After the flags of republics and empires have been blown to tatters, and the earth itself has tasted death, the church of Jesus shall stand forth glorious, free from blemish and mark of decay, the gates of Hades shall not prevail against it. Therefore, my beloved brethren, in these confused and confusing days, be steadfast, immovable in the presence of the world's clamor and rancor, always building your life and the lives of as many as God intrusts to your keeping, into the church of the Lord, forasmuch as you know that such labor is not in vain in the Lord.

LECTURE II

BUILDING THE BROTHERHOOD

BUILDING THE BROTHERHOOD

"Brotherhood" is St. Peter's name for the church. The conception of the church held by the leader of the Twelve and the man to whom our Lord first promised the keys of the Kingdom is deserving of sustained attention. That members of the church are brothers, St. Peter everywhere takes for granted. "Be ye all like-minded, compassionate, loving as brothers, tender-hearted, humble-minded" — this sums up his idea of the disposition which church members should have toward one another. He has many bits of advice to give his converts, but this is chief: "Above all things be fervent in your love among yourselves. Honor all men. Love the brotherhood."

St. John holds the same conception. To him the church is a band of brothers, and the first duty of church members is loving one another. There is little else that the beloved apostle cares to write. "He that loveth his brother abideth in the light." "We know that we have passed out of death into life because we love the brethren." "We ought

43

to lay down our lives for the brethren." "This is his commandment, that we should believe in the name of his son Jesus Christ, and love one another." "Beloved, let us love one another." "If God so loved us we also ought to love one another." "If a man say, I love God and hateth his brother, he is a liar ; for he that loveth not his brother whom he hath seen, cannot love God whom he hath not seen." "This commandment have we from him that he who loveth God, love his brother also." With St. John's writings before us, it is easy to believe the tradition that when he was old, unable any longer to walk, the young men in the church in Ephesus were wont to carry him before the people, to whom he repeated again and again, "Little children, love one another." When they asked him why he said this so many times, his reply was, "Because it is the Lord's precept, and if only it be done, it is enough."

St. Paul was not in the upper chamber when the Twelve received the new commandment, but his conception of the church is identical with that of John and Peter. To Paul the church is a brotherhood. "Concerning love of the brethren," Paul writes to the church in Thessalonica, "ye have no need that one write unto you, for ye yourselves are taught of God to love one another; for indeed ye do it toward all the brethren which are in all Macedonia. But we exhort you, brethren, that ye abound more and more." This is his exhortation to all Christians and he gives expression to it again and again, "In love of the brethren be tenderly affectioned one to another; in honor preferring one another." It is only as Christians are rooted and grounded in love that they are "strong to apprehend with all the saints what is the breadth and length and height and depth, and to know the love of Christ which passeth knowledge." In his first letter to the Corinthians, Paul's conception of love breaks into language of unsurpassed and unforgettable splendor. He declares what love is, how it acts, feels, thinks, and what victories it wins. Without it, no matter what else we possess, we have nothing. This was written to the church which was most deficient in that which is the distinctive treasure of a Christian church. Unless a church is a brotherhood, a company of men and women whose sympathies and purposes are intertwined, and whose lives are interlaced and blended, we may call it a Christian church, but it does not bear in the body of its life the marks of the Lord Jesus.

Whence did these three preachers get their conception of the church ? They preached only what they received. It was Jesus' habit to remind his disciples that he was their Master and that all they were brethren. The crowning period of his life was devoted almost exclusively to the task of knitting together the hearts of the men who were to constitute the nucleus of his church. How heavy this burden lay upon his heart is seen in his behavior and words in the upper chamber. All along the way that day, there had been outbreaks of temper on the part of the twelve, and the old spirit of ill-will crops out again as they take their places round the table. The feast cannot go on. Christ can hold no festival except where hearts are sweet. He takes a basin and a towel and proceeds to bathe the disciples' feet, not because he cares for the dust on their feet, but because he is pained by the estrangement of their hearts. This done, he announces a commandment which is to take precedence over all the instructions which he has hitherto given them. "A new commandment I give unto you, that ye love one another ; even as I have loved you, that ye also love one another. By this shall all men know that ye are my disciples, if ye have love one to another." This is indeed startling teaching. Let all who would preach the gospel read, mark, learn, and inwardly digest it. The distinctive note of the Christian life is here proclaimed to be love for one's fellow-Christians. A man proves himself a Christian, not by loving men in general, but by loving his brethren in Christ. The first and inevitable fruit of an instructed Christian heart is love for one's brother Christians. This is a truth which our Lord labored unceasingly to make clear to his disciples. The things which are uppermost in one's mind are likely to come out in his prayers. They are sure to emerge in the prayers which one offers in the presence of death. Listen then to the last prayer of Jesus. He prays that his disciples may be one. He prays for it again and again. It is the one longing which throbs through his whole prayer. The outside world passes for a season out of his thought. The nations and their needs sink below the horizon. He thinks only of his church, of the men who are there in his presence, and of the multitudes who will believe on him through their word. He can conceive of no higher blessing for them than communion of spirit, comradeship in heart, union in love. "That they may all be one, even as thou Father art in me and I in thee, that they also may be one in us : that the

world may believe that thou didst send me."
Fellowship, then, is to be the proof of the divine
power of Jesus, evidence to the world that he came
from heaven. The world is not to be convinced and
converted by reasoning or philosophy or eloquence,
but by the love of Christians for one another.
"The glory which thou hast given me I have given
unto them; that they may be one, even as we are
one; I in them, and thou in me, that they may be
perfected into one: that the world may know that
thou didst send me, and lovedst them, even as thou
lovedst me." This is amazing doctrine. It sounds
novel even now. Christ declares his mission to be
the binding of men together by indissoluble bonds.
It is by the brotherliness of those who believe in
Jesus that the hard heart of the world is to be
softened and the truthfulness of Jesus' words
established. The world is to be brought to God
by Christians loving one another.

It is incontrovertible that, according to the New
Testament, the men who were baptized into the
spirit of Jesus looked upon the church from the
beginning as a brotherhood or family. The vocabulary and customs of home life were carried over into
the church. The church was known as the household of faith, the family of God. Christians called

one another not "Christians," but "brethren," and after the fashion of Eastern lands they greeted one another at their meetings with a kiss. In their assemblies they gathered round a common table, enjoying a love-feast together. The sacrament of the Lord's Supper was linked to the dinner table, the central social institution in the home. The church's most sacred ceremony was a reminder that believers belong to one another. The church was a communion of brothers. High in the list of graces stood the grace of hospitality. Christians when they travelled were never to find themselves away from home. All congregations of believers were to be bound together by sacred and spiritual ties, and thus was the Lord's prayer to be fulfilled. A favorite name for "church" in the early Christian centuries was "Brotherhood." Alas, that it was ever lost!

When we close the New Testament and look around us, we find ourselves in a different world. There is a change in the atmosphere which is chilling. The Roman Catholic idea of the church is not the idea of Peter. Her definition of the church as phrased by Cardinal Bellarmine is: "The one and true church is the congregation of men united by the profession of the same Christian faith and the communion of the same sacraments under

E

the rule of the legitimate pastors, and especially the one vicar of Christ upon earth." Everything mentioned in this definition is external. Love has no stated place at all. In Roman Catholic practice the church is essentially a hierarchy, the officials being exalted far above the laity, constituting a class apart, while the rank and file of the Lord's followers, often reduced to the level of mere spectators, come to God only through the hierarchy. How different Christian history would have been, if from the fourth to the sixteenth century the men who claimed to sit in Peter's chair had followed Peter, and had said to all priests: "Tend the flock of God, exercising the oversight, not of constraint, but willingly, according unto God; nor yet for filthy lucre, but of a ready mind; neither as lording it over the charge allotted to you, but making yourselves ensamples to the flock," and to all congregations, "Love as brethren, have fervent love among yourselves, love the brotherhood."

Nor has Protestantism ever read with unclouded eye what the New Testament says about the church. The definition formulated by the Anglican church and adopted by the Protestant Episcopal and Methodist Episcopal churches reads thus: "The visible church of Christ is a congregation of faithful men, in the which the pure word of God is preached, and the sacraments be duly administered according to Christ's ordinance, in all those things that of necessity are requisite to the same." The Westminster Confession says : "The Catholic or universal church, which is invisible, consists of the whole number of the elect that have been, are, or shall be gathered into one, under Christ, the head thereof ; and is the spouse, the body, the fulness of him that filleth all in all. The visible church, which is also catholic or universal under the gospel, consists of all those throughout the world, that profess the true religion, and of their children ; and is the kingdom of the Lord Jesus Christ, the house and family of God, out of which there is no ordinary possibility of salvation." These definitions reappear with minor variations in most of the creeds of Protestant christendom. The two features of the church which Protestants have made conspicuous are the preaching of the word and the administration of the sacraments. But preaching is not sufficient to make a church, nor is the proper administration of the sacraments. That a definition of the church should have in it no reference to what the Head of the church counts fundamental is indeed calami-

tous. When did Jesus magnify sacraments and
sermons, passing by the obligations and ministries
of love? The alleged "one vicar of Christ upon
earth" does not make a church, nor does a bishop,
nor a preacher, nor a man who baptizes, nor an
official who offers a prayer over the bread and the
wine. A church is a brotherhood, a school for
training in fellowship, a home for the cultivation
of the social virtues and the human graces, a society
in which men are bound together in sympathy and
holy service by a common allegiance to the Son of
God. It is a congregation of faithful men, ever
striving to learn and live the new commandment,
looking unto Jesus for power to understand and
practice the law of love. The new commandment
is the standard by which all churches must be
measured, and in the light of this standard the
church universal knows herself to be poor and blind
and naked. Many city churches are made up of
people who do not even know one another, and
who do not want to know one another. Too many
village churches are composed of people who know
one another, and are sorry that they do. The
very thing which the New Testament asserts to
be the one thing needful, and without which the
world cannot be won for Christ, is the thing which

is to-day least abundant.   To create an ampler and
a warmer fellowship inside the church of Jesus is the
first work for which preachers are ordained, and
yet many of them, instead of staying at home and
attending to their business, have gone scampering
off in wild crusades against the distant Saracens,
wasting their strength in frenzied efforts to reconstruct by a furious blowing of trumpets the economic
and social order.   There are many congregations, let
us be thankful, in which the new commandment is
understood and honored, and it is these congregations which constitute the hope of Christendom.
They hold in their hand the key which unlocks all
the doors.   They possess the secret for which the
world is waiting.   No churches, let us hope, are
altogether devoid of the love for which the Master
and his apostles pleaded.   Even in congregations
which seem paralyzed or dead, there is usually
at the centre a little circle of loyal and devoted
believers, whose hearts have been fused by the
Holy Spirit, and whose lives have been blended by
fellowship in Christian work and prayer.   To
extend this circle of lovers, whether it be larger or
smaller, and endow it with a fuller measure of wisdom and power is, in my judgment, the distinctive
and crucial work of the Christian minister.   It is

the work which the Master did, and he says, "Follow me !"

There are probably few important sentences in the gospels used so seldom by Christian ministers as texts for sermons as is the golden sentence of our Lord : "Love one another, even as I have loved you." It seems to be a difficult sentence to find, and even more difficult to understand. It is often made to mean something different from what it teaches. A common interpretation makes it equivalent to "love all men everywhere." But such an exposition empties it of its content, and robs it of its power to accomplish the work which Jesus had in mind. He is not exhorting here to a vague humanitarianism or a wholesale philanthropy. He is not proclaiming the brotherhood of man. He is not thinking of men in general. He is speaking to members of his church, and telling them how to live together so as to convince the world that he is what he claims to be. Victory for his cause is to be achieved by their love for one another. It is no ordinary love which is called for, but love fashioned after his own, and lifted to its white intensity and heavenly temper. A Christian owes something to a fellow-Christian which he owes to no other human being, his first duty is to his fellow-believers, his first obligation is to his Christian brethren, his first concern is with his comrades in Christ. It is by Christians loving one another after the sacrificial manner of Jesus that other men are to become Christians. Love is the law of the church. Love is the badge of discipleship. Love is the chief evangelist and head worker. Love is the power which overcomes. It is not love for the community or love for humanity, but love for one's fellow-Christians by which the door of the world's heart is to be opened. The teaching was plain and the early Christians caught it. The secret of the progress of the early church lies revealed in the exclamation of the pagan crowd — "Behold how these Christians love one another!"

The primary work of a preacher, then, is the cultivation by word and deed of the spirit of Christlike brotherliness among the members of his own church. Many ministers shrink from this work as something narrowing and unworthy. The very statement that such is a minister's work sounds like heresy and arouses antagonism and revulsion in many hearts. Such teaching seems like harking back to the dark ages. The brotherhood of man and not the brotherhood of Christians is the doctrine which our century is ready to hear.

All men are our brothers. A man who is up to date will make no distinctions but will love everybody alike. Let a preacher, therefore, exhort his people continually to love humanity, being careful to lay no special emphasis, as a New Testament writer mistakenly did, upon those who belong to the household of faith. It is just here that many a minister makes his greatest mistake. In his eagerness to be broad he becomes narrow. In ignoring limitations prescribed by the Lord of life he becomes feeble. By trying to do too much he achieves nothing. In his liberality he wipes out distinctions which cannot be repudiated without loss. In his zeal to rise above boundaries, he loses himself in the clouds. Nothing is more essential to a preacher in our day than an understanding of the function and power of limitations. It is only as a man is willing to confine himself within narrow limits that he can do any mighty work. Men all round us are frittering away their lives because of their vagueness. Sermons in appalling numbers amount to little because of their generalities. Definiteness in thought and action is the thing above all things for the twentieth century preacher to cultivate. Concentration is the supreme prudence of ministerial life. It is easy to declaim eloquently about the brotherhood of man, but much that is said upon that subject is vapid and futile. The air is full of talk about brotherhood, but brotherhood does not come by poetic quotations and rhapsodical orating. Brotherhood is a spiritual creation, the work of men who have been recreated in Christ. It is a fellowship of souls based upon a fellowship with God's only-begotten Son. The redemption of the world is carried onward by the binding of Christian hearts and lives together. To Paul, fellowship was everything. His letters were full of it because his heart was overflowing. To get the members of the local church closer together, and the churches of each region closer together, and the churches of the Jewish and Gentile worlds closer together — this was the object of his labors and prayers. Christianity to him is fellowship in the Lord. Without fellowship faith is empty, hope is darkened, love is starved. It is through the communion of saints that this world and all worlds are to see what God is and what he is able to do.

Do not be afraid, then, to preach boldly the doctrine of the new commandment. Preach it just as the Lord himself taught it. Count it your joy to train the members of your church in the fine art of living together. It is the most difficult of all the arts, and the church is the school ordained of God for perfecting men in this art. You are not doing a narrow work when you teach the members of your church the range and wealth of Christian fellowship. The church is the world in miniature. In it exist all the forces and relationships, the entanglements and evils, which the world as a whole presents. There is not a world evil which can be anywhere so effectively attacked as within the church of Christ. There is not an industrial or social or racial problem which can be dealt with outside so profoundly as inside the Christian brotherhood. When you straighten out the tangled relations of your church members to one another, you are contributing to the solution of social problems everywhere. When you soften class antipathies and racial antagonisms within your congregation, you are helping to solve the most baffling of the world complications. When you induce all sorts and conditions of men to live together as brethren in your own church communion, you are hastening the day when men the wide world over shall be brothers. Humanity is in the making, and the church is the institution in which society is moulded into nobler forms and fitted for finer issues. When Paul built a slave into the brotherhood at Colossæ, he signed the death warrant for slavery in England and America. When Jesus induced twelve men differing from one another widely in temperament, idea, and social standing to sit down together in an upper chamber in Jerusalem, he contributed to the solution of the social problem in every city throughout the world. It is impossible to kindle a fire on your church hearth without the world feeling the warmth of it. But you cannot kindle a fire unless you bring the fagots together. The minister's first business is to get his people together. Let him preach to his church, and his church, when converted, will preach to the world. Let him kindle the church, and the church will illumine the community. The lamp of the town is the church. If the lamp of the church is darkness, how great is that darkness!

The minister who gives himself to the training of a church in Christian fellowship is not dwarfing the affections or curtailing the range of the sympathies of his people. He is creating the very capacities and powers by means of which Christ's large wish for the world can be most speedily fulfilled. Affections are most surely enriched and strengthened only when cultivated in narrow fields. It is the man who loves his own wife as he loves no other woman, who comes to take a chivalric attitude to all

women everywhere. By his love for one woman
he grows into a widening appreciation of the dignity
and beauty of womanhood. It is the father who
loves his own children as he loves no others, whose
affections go out farthest toward all boys and girls
and who is swiftest to gather them into the round
tower of his heart. Men who are most faithful to
their own homes are the men to be first counted on
for the defence and maintenance of the interests of
all homes. It is the man who has come into fellowship with his brother men in his own Church who is
most likely to come into right relations with men
who have no connection with organized Christianity. Love when once kindled travels far, but it
must first be kindled. The church of Jesus is established for the express purpose of kindling the
fire of love. Sermons are a part of the fuel by which
the fire is nourished. Pastoral work also feeds and
safeguards the holy flame. The wise preacher is always striving to bring the members of his church
into a richer fellowship. The weakness of the
modern church lies in its dwarfed affections. The
shame of present-day Christianity is its stunted
sympathies. The church is rich in money, ideas,
apparatus, numbers, but poor in love. This is in
part the fault of preachers. Too many of them

fail to cultivate the affections. They do not understand how to open the heart. They are interested in problems and what they call the "Kingdom," but they are not sufficiently interested in the group of people of whom they are the appointed religious teachers. They neglect the work of interlacing lives, of binding men into bundles, of twining purposes and sympathies together for the advancement of Christ's glory. There are congregations which have scant sympathy with the outside world, because their members have meagre sympathy with one another. If sympathy is cultivated inside the church, it spills over into the outside world. There are churches which have no interest in the struggles and hopes of wage-earners, largely because there is no interest among the members of those churches in one another. Christian love is expressed in the hymn-book, but does not exist in the hearts of the people who sing the hymns; and not loving the man by his side, it is impossible for the loveless church member to love the man who is far away. When love is kindled in the hearts of church members for one another, it is a fire which burns its way to the end of the world. Not a little of the indifference of many Christians to the work of foreign missions is due to their atrophied social

sympathies. Their social nature has become enfeebled, and by neglecting their obligations to their
fellow-townsmen, they find it impossible to respond
to the claims of unknown men on the other side of the
globe. Their lack of the spirit of brotherly affection
incapacitates them also for the worship of God.
Their worship is mechanical and unsatisfying.
The secret of this was told long ago by a man who
laid it down as axiomatic, that if a man does not
love his brother whom he has seen he cannot love
God whom he has not seen. It is the very quintes-
sence of the Christian teaching that we can know
God only through man, that we come to God only
through man, and that we worship God best by
loving men. Many a preacher has tried to put
warmth into the worship of his church, and all
in vain, because he did not know that the source of
warmth is human fellowship, and that the place to
begin working for an enrichment of the devotional
spirit is not among his books, elaborating arguments
going to prove that men ought to delight in the
worship of God, but in the social meeting where
church members come to know one another.
Christians who are interested in one another invariably become more interested in God. Loving
men is the only way to grow in the grace of loving

God.   Unless a church is socialized, how can it be expected to feel an interest in social movements? A set of people who are not interested in one another will not be likely in the house of prayer to worship God with glad and exultant hearts, or in the field of Christian service to work effectively for the advancement of the kingdom.   The preacher's first work is the building of a brotherhood.   Out of this, when once created, all sorts of reviving streams will flow.

These are good times for preachers to ponder the meaning of the new commandment and to train their people in the practice of it.   Men are thinking as never before of solidarity, and organic life and corporate responsibilities.   In the commercial world there is an amazing revelation of the power of co-operation, in the industrial world a growing apprehension of the possibilities of collectivism, in the new psychology a deepened insight into the relation of personality to society.   There is a world-wide movement called Socialism.   In all the kingdoms of life there is a new vision of the meaning of social relationships and the miracle-working power of combinations.   In the whole trend of the world's thought, the Spirit of God is saying something to the churches, and the preacher who has ears to hear will receive a revelation. We are living in a social age and the question at the front is the social question. Man's social nature is unprecedentedly alive and is clamoring for a satisfaction which cannot be denied it. Men are massing themselves in cities, not chiefly because they are most needed there, or because they can secure work there, but because they find in city life gratification for their social cravings. Men hunger for companionship. They have discovered that it is not good for them to live alone. Solitude is unendurable, isolation is death. As soon as men come together they organize, gather themselves into groups, form fraternities, unions, leagues, clubs. Men live by fellowship. It is only when hearts and hands come together that existence passes into life. The multiplication of societies, therefore, goes on increasingly. This is a fact of which every alert preacher is bound to take notice. Many a preacher has already observed it to his consternation. He has found the unions and lodges, granges and clubs, swallowing up the men of the community, leaving for the church only women and children. In bitterness of spirit he has cried out against these secular organizations, denouncing them as enemies of the church of God. But all such denunciation is futile. One cannot change the movement of the tides. Man is a social animal. God made him such. Men are made for fellowship, and if they do not find it in the church of God, they will seek it where it may be found. The wise preacher will waste no time in hurling thunderbolts at rival organizations, but will set to work with both hands to strengthen the church where the church to-day is weakest. His ambition will be to make his church the warmest and most effective brotherhood in all the town. No stranger member shall remain ungreeted. No unfortunate member shall go unbefriended. No invalid shall be unvisited. No needy person shall be unassisted. No bewildered soul shall go unadvised. No home of mourning shall be neglected. No act of needed mercy shall be omitted. The church shall be a home. Men cannot live by sermons alone, but by every word which proceeds out of the mouth of God. One of God's choice words is fellowship, and unless a church offers fellowship it is doomed. Worship without fellowship is contrary to nature. The worship in the New Testament is carried on by brothers. Men cannot love a church if all it offers is the privilege of listening to sermons and paying pew rent. It is the comradeship of college life which makes men

F

love their college. Their devotion to their **Alma Mater** springs out of the friendships formed during their student days. The abstract truths taught by learned professors will not account for that undying affection which many a man feels for his college. His heart is warm because it is bound up with other hearts. A man's love for his church depends in large measure upon the relationship established between himself and his fellow-members. The friendships formed in church life and work are among the most sacred and enduring into which the soul of man can come. Unless a man enters into the social life of the church, he is practically not a member of it at all. Listening to a preacher speak on religious topics every Sunday does not make one a church member, even though his name is written on the church roll. Fellowship is of the essence of church membership, and to cultivate and enrich this fellowship is the primary task of the Christian preacher.

A sharp distinction ought to be made between a church and an audience. It is to be regretted that we have come to rank churches by the size of their nominal membership, and to judge preachers by the number of persons who listen to their sermons. A superficial man is consequently tempted to work, not for a church, but for an audience.   An audience, however, is not worth working for.   An audience is a set of unrelated people drawn together by a short-lived attraction, an agglomeration of individuals finding themselves together for a brief time. It is a fortuitous concourse of human atoms, scattering as soon as a certain performance is ended.   It is a pile of leaves to be blown away by the wind, a handful of sand lacking consistency and cohesion, a number of human filings drawn into position by a pulpit magnet, and which will drop away as soon as the magnet is removed.   An audience is a crowd, a church is a family.   An audience is a gathering, a church is a fellowship.   An audience is a collection, a church is an organism.   An audience is a heap of stones, a church is a temple.   Preachers are ordained, not to attract an audience, but to build a church. Coarse and ambitious and worldly men, if richly gifted, can draw audiences.   Only a disciple of the Lord can build a church.   It is not uncommon for a supposedly mighty church to wilt like Jonah's gourd, as soon as the man in the pulpit vanishes.   The structure was of hay and wood and stubble, and it disappeared in the fire of God's swift judgment day.

It is because so many churches are audiences, rather than brotherhoods, that thousands of

Christians on changing their place of residence drop out of church connections altogether. Their old church membership meant nothing to them, and therefore membership in another church has no attraction for them. When they joined the church, it was the minister who welcomed them. The church took no note of their advent. When death visited their home, it was the pastor who offered condolence. The church was not grieved by the bereavement. When a financial crisis swept the little fortune away, leaving the world dark, it was the preacher who spoke a sympathetic word, but the church cared for none of these things. When the hour for departure arrived, it was the head official of the church who said, "Good-by," but the brotherhood had nothing whatever to say. This is the tragedy which goes on in hundreds of parishes, and so long as it continues many preachers must preach to dwindling congregations and the church must limp like a giant, not with a wounded heel, but with a broken leg. A man who has been starved in one church is not likely to connect himself with another. When he makes for himself a new home, he will identify himself with a society which offers him comradeship and furnishes an atmosphere in which his soul can live.

The problem of developing new converts is even more perplexing than that of retaining the allegiance of old ones. It is easier to convert men than it is to educate them. The converts are many, but the developed workers are few. In a season of spiritual awakening ten seem to be healed, but when the preacher goes in search of them, he cries in bewilderment, "Where are the nine?" Only a small proportion of those who start the Christian life ever reach spiritual maturity. One of the reasons is a deadly environment. The atmosphere is so cold that the young convert is fatally chilled. He gasps for a few months and then expires. There are many congregations in which church obligations are so little known and practised that it is only the exceptional convert who survives the early stages of Christian discipleship. The atmosphere of the church has in it no life-giving qualities. The church is not a brotherhood, and when a new recruit starts to follow Jesus, he is not cheered by brotherly voices or guided by fraternal hands. In the darkness of the first days, there is no one to do what Ananias did for Saul when he laid his warm hand on the trembling convert's head, saying, "Brother Saul, receive thy sight." It is often the touch of a brother's hand which opens the heavens to the

beginning Christian. In successful church work
the voice of the preacher must be supplemented
by the welcoming hand of a brother. The preacher
is never sufficient when he stands alone. Peter was
mighty on the day of Pentecost, because one hundred and twenty — the entire brotherhood — stood
with him. The Bible is not enough to make men
strong. Human hands and hearts are needed.
The revelation which came through holy men of
old must be completed by a revelation coming
through men now living. The human hand has a
power which even the Scriptures do not possess.
There is something in a human heart which completes the power of Almighty God in the work of
saving men. Eloquence is a force, but affection is
a force still more potent. Social intercourse is a
means of grace as truly as are prayer and the sacraments, and is of equal rank with these. Warmth
is as essential as light in the growing of souls. The
preacher may furnish light, but the bulk of the
heat must be supplied by the brotherhood. The
finest and deepest powers of the soul are called into
play only by social contact. Every point of contact
— or, as Paul puts it, "every joint" — is a channel
of divine grace. It is at the points where Christian
lives touch that there springs up the life by which

the church is nourished and made capable for her work. God's grace flows through social bonds. We are held in our place by personal attachments. We save one another. This is why Paul is always exhorting his converts to subject themselves one to another. He is not satisfied at times with his figure of a temple. He supplements it with his figure of the body. Church members are even closer together than the stones of a temple wall. They are knit together like the parts of an organism. Each organ exists for the life and prosperity of the whole. Each is needed by all. The whole is dependent on each. The preacher is impotent without the assistance of the brotherhood. His words will never catch fire unless the brotherhood creates the atmosphere in which gospel truths blaze. He cannot, unassisted, hold his converts. It is impossible for him, single-handed, to keep his spiritual children from falling. His success in conserving the fruits of his labors will be measured by his ability to build and maintain a compact and conquering brotherhood. Many a sermon must be preached on the duties which Christians owe to one another. Many an hour must be devoted to the difficult and delicate work of linking the lives of the new converts into the lives of those who have travelled farther along the perilous and glorious way.

Building the brotherhood, this is our work, and work more taxing and baffling God has never given to mortals. It brought the Son of God to the cross, and every man who attempts the same work must drink of a like cup and be baptized with a similar baptism. Not until a minister strives to build a brotherhood does he realize how unsocial human nature is, how narrow and how cold. Not till then does he discover what havoc sin has wrought, and what low and crude conceptions of the obligations of Christian discipleship lodge in many a Christian heart. It is only then that human nature begins to reveal its deeper uglinesses and that many interior littlenesses and meannesses come trooping into the light. Even the Lord himself could not get twelve men to sit together at a table on the last night of his life on earth without an exhibition of petty irritation and wounded vanity which cast a deeper shadow over his already breaking heart. It is comparatively easy for most Christians to listen to sermons. This lays slight strain on Christian character. It is easy for many Christians to give money. Some of them will give it generously. It is not difficult to persuade certain of the elect to engage in Christian work. Work among the submerged has in many places become even fashionable. But for church members to be brotherly with one another, this is indeed difficult, in many quarters apparently impossible. Men teach boys in mission schools who cannot be·induced to show an interest in their younger brethren in their own church. Women work for women in a settlement or mission who will not recognize women of a different social station in their own church family. Men make contributions for carrying the gospel into foreign lands who act like heathen in their home church. To the amazement of the young preacher, social estrangements flourish inside the company of the sanctified. Class antagonisms do not soften under the most fervent preaching of the gospel. Racial lines remain straight and fixed, and all the rivalries and enmities, vanities and prejudices, of which the world is full, grow rank inside the garden of the Lord. Possibly it is for this reason that certain preachers devote so much attention to sinners outside their congregations. A man finds relief in striking at a distant octopus who has been discomfited by some unregenerate pigmy within his reach. The sinners inside his parish are so hopeless that in sheer desperation the defeated preacher gives his attention to the great outside world, whose tragedies it is easy to portray, whose colossal culprits it is harmless to castigate, and concerning whose reconstruction it is refreshing to give advice.

But the servant of the Master must not follow the things which are easy. Let him take hold of the things which are hard. Let him lay both hands on his church. He may find that his church is after all only an audience, and that its members need to be fused into a body which the Lord can use. It may be that the older people are not interested in the younger people and that they eye each other across a chasm which widens and deepens with the years. Possibly employers have steadfastly held aloof from wage-earners, and the rich men have never shown friendliness for the men who are poor. It may be that the new members have been allowed to continue strangers, and that older members have sat for years within six feet of each other without even so much as a look of mutual recognition. Possibly there are men who quarrelled ten years ago, and who have doggedly resisted every suggestion of reconciliation. They do not speak either in the church or on the street, and this ill-will festering in their hearts poisons the atmosphere of the whole

church. Here is a problem more urgent for the
minister than any of the disputes between labor
and capital. It may be that members of the church
are estranged from one another by differences in
doctrinal opinion. An orthodox brother thinks
that his orthodoxy gives him a right to malign those
who differ from him, and in defending the truth
he tramples the new commandment under his feet.
To train Christian men to love one another who
differ from one another theologically, is a task
more formidable than converting the toughest
of the publicans and the trickiest of the sinners.
But Jesus is explicit on this point. Worship must
wait on reconciliation. Get right with your brother,
says the Lord of love, before you set up your altar.
It may be that some Pharaoh has grown up in the
midst of the congregation who lords it over both the
minister and the saints. He has made trouble for
years, and, unless suppressed, he will make trouble
for years to come. Such a man must be dealt with.
His sin is as destructive to the life of the church as
habitual drunkenness or flagrant lust. Unbrotherly
conduct in a church member always makes him a fit
subject for church discipline, and the minister is not
doing his duty who allows the church to be torn and
harassed by an ungodly despot who has set up his

throne in the parish. Nothing worth while could go on in the upper chamber until Judas was got rid of, and so in many a church the communion should not be celebrated again until the confirmed mischief-maker has been cast out. Patience and mercy are always in order, but there are certain transgressors who are apparently incorrigible, and their way ought to be made hard.

These are the arduous and cardinal things which a minister has to do. It is easy to denounce sins in general and still easier to unfold beautiful ideas, but to induce different classes of church members to live and work together as Christians — this is the most stupendous and heart-breaking labor to which a minister of the Gospel can set himself. The church of Christ if not a brotherhood is a failure. To make it a brotherhood, this is the hope and despair of the minister, this is his cross and his crown. To build all types of humanity into this brotherhood is an aim never to be lost sight of. Churches organized along social lines are breeders of mischief. A church made up of people of but one social grade is a church doomed to a blasted spiritual experience. A church of the rich is not a church after the ideal of Jesus, neither is a church of the poor. It is only when the rich and the poor sit down together that they come to believe that the Lord is the maker of them all. A church exists for the express purpose of knitting together the lives of those whom the forces of the world have driven asunder. The rich and the poor are to come together at the feet of him who, once rich, for man's sake became poor. The laborer and the capitalist are to join hands in front of the cross. The cultivated man and the man without schooling are to learn each other's worth in Christian service. The foreigners are to be no more aliens, but full members of the family of God. Brotherhood is what the world is clamoring for, and it is an example of brotherhood which the Christian church must give. The church is the laboratory in which experiments in brotherliness are to be conducted first and farthest. The church is the factory in which men are to be converted into brothers. A man with a brotherly heart is a form of power which the industrial and commercial worlds are waiting for. That church is doing humanity the largest service which develops within itself the highest potencies of love.

Let preachers, then, create in their churches by their preaching the spirit of love, and the churches will pass it on. The world will never listen to ser-

mons on sympathy and good-will until these exist in
heavenly abundance inside the church. What is
the use of preachers trying to give the world a theory
of something which the church itself does not practise? No man can preach love effectively over the
body of a loveless church. Our immediate task
is not to Christianize the world, but to Christianize
the church. The church progressively Christianized
will gradually Christianize society. God cuts our
piece of work small in order that we may do it well.
The task, though limited, is dynamic and far-
reaching. The church, if leaven, will leaven the
whole lump. Our first business is not with the
lump, but with the leaven. He is the greatest
preacher who so frames and utters the thoughts
of God as to bind together the largest number of
Christian hearts in closest fellowship for Christlike
service.

LECTURE III

BUILDING THE INDIVIDUAL

BUILDING THE INDIVIDUAL

HAVING viewed the style and proportions of the edifice, let us consider the living stones which are to go into it. After looking at the whole, it is time to study the parts. The fault of the old individualism was that it began with the individual and ended with him. It worked upon the single man, with no clear social end in view. Christian individualism begins with a social vision. It sees that the individual exists in and for society, and that personality feeds and completes itself only in the group. The living stones have no abiding life, unless built into the walls of a growing temple. The preacher must be an individualist, but he must see in his mind's eye the completed building, before he begins to shape the stones out of which the edifice is to be constructed.

Because of its lack of the social vision, individualism is to-day discredited, and the danger is that in casting aside an individualism which is defective, we may throw away the individualism which is Christian. Aggregated life has become so important in our eyes, that the temptation is to lose interest in the human unit. The social vision has for a season shaken our faith in the individualistic method. A thousand voices remind us that the world is the subject of redemption, that society as a whole must be claimed for Christ, that the church is not a rescue ship, picking up isolated individuals tossed on the angry billows, but a mighty servant of the Lord gathering up the total interests and institutions of the entire race of men. Stirred by these imperial phrases, not a few have grown distrustful of all traditional methods, and are thinking of men exclusively in masses. Communities and classes and races are alone large enough to catch and hold attention. It is not any one rich man or any one poor man, but rather the rich and the poor, upon whom the gaze of the world is fastened. It is capital and labor, rather than any one capitalist or any one laborer, which presents a problem that appeals to the modern mind. Many leaders and teachers have a lively concern for the races, white, black, yellow, and brown, who care little for the individual representatives of those races. It is not uncommon to lose sight of men altogether and fix the eyes on the economic system, the industrial and social order. Rescuing individuals here and there seems a puttering and paltry occupation, and to alter the structure of society, the framework of the world, is counted the only business worthy the efforts of a full-statured, far-visioned man.

Preaching in many pulpits has grown increasingly impersonal. Sermons have become more and more discussions of social questions. To urge upon the individuals in the congregation an immediate surrender to Christ as Lord, seems to certain preachers somewhat irrelevant, and to others quite ill-mannered. It is a problem-loving age, as the magazines and plays and novels testify, and it is hardly to be wondered at that the pulpit should be swept along into this roaring torrent. The subjects uppermost in current literature climb into the pulpit, and before the preacher is aware of it he has become a professor of economics, a lecturer on sociology, a writer of pulpit editorials, a social reformer, a clerical philanthropist, an instructor in the literature of modern movements, or a practitioner of the art of mental healing. His favorite subjects are Trades-unionism, Socialism, Immigration, Child Labor, Juvenile Courts, Democracy, Industrialism, Sanitation, Labor and Capital, Trusts and Syndicates, Factory Legislation, Civic Reform, Overcrowding, Sewerage, Sweatshops, Conservation of

National Resources, Woman Suffrage, Christian Science, and Old Age Pensions. Men all around him are discussing these matters, and the preacher feels that he also must make his contribution. The individual counts less and less, the world looms more and more. The preacher is interested in man, but not in men, in humanity, but not in the particular persons into whose faces he looks on the Lord's day.

The scientific doctrine of environment has also been operative in shaping the pattern of pulpit teaching. One of the most potent factors in moulding a man's life is undoubtedly his surroundings, and science has emphasized and popularized this fact. The preacher in his parish finds many evidences that environment is mighty, and this discovery when duly pondered is sure to modify and may revolutionize his whole outlook on life. He strives to elevate a man in the slums, and fails. He makes up his mind that to save a man in a swamp is impossible. The swamp itself must first be drained. Disease cannot be kept from the home when the atmosphere for a mile around is charged with poison germs. The first thing to do is to cleanse the air. He is tempted to forsake the individual altogether, feeling that the first work must be done upon the city as a whole. He begins to doubt the doctrine of personal responsibility, and to lay the blame for vicious lives upon society. The social order becomes to him the transgressor; the economic system, the mother of criminals. Until these have been changed, pass condemnation, he says, on no man. You cannot redeem the individual until you change the structure of the world. This is the style of reasoning by which men of tender hearts and impatient tempers are sometimes carried into one of the many camps of Socialism. Socialism fascinates because it offers to do things on a vast scale, and in the telling of its story uses only words which are passionate and vivid. Why should a man squander his energy in pulling an occasional mortal out of his misery, when, by uniting with other men, he can help to throw the whole framework of civilization in the twinkling of an eye on the junk-heap? It is not uncommon for preachers whose social conscience is sensitive to convert their sermons into chambers of horrors. Sunday gives them an opportunity to uncover the world's ulcers and running sores. Their sense of the world's need and the impetuosity of their temper render them impatient with the old method of faithful dealing with the individual man.

One man in their sight counts for nothing.   What is
he?   A straw blown by the gale, a fly on the rim
of one of the wheels of the world's chariot, a grain of
sand on an illimitable shore, a bubble on the crest
of an immeasurable billow, a vapor that appears for
a little time and then vanishes away.   The religious
leader who is wise — so these men think — will
direct his sermons to the community; his effort will
be to reconstruct the order of the world.

It is unfortunate that this argument should be so
plausible as to seduce many sympathetic and conscientious minds, for it is certainly fallacious and
when acted on leads to an impoverishment of pulpit
power.   Many a man is preaching to a dwindling
congregation because his sermons have lost the
personal note.   He chills by his vague generalities,
or enrages by his wholesale denunciations.   A congregation is to be pitied if it has in the pulpit a clerical Hamlet whose every second sermon is a lamen-
tation that the time is out of joint, leaving his
people to infer that he was born to set it right.
Such a man would be saved from his aberrations
by looking steadily at the individuals immediately
before him.   The preacher who allows his eye to
wander long from the individual man is destined to
lose power as a preacher.   That man preaches

most searchingly, most persuasively, and most effectively who knows best and loves most the individual.

This is not an age in which the preacher can afford to lose out of his work the personal touch. Many forces are conspiring to blur the edges of individuality and melt men down into a common mass. The immediate effect of the teaching of modern science is to create a loneliness in the human heart. Her revelation of the vastness of the universe beats man down into a feeling of insignificance, and brings to the lips with a fresh poignancy the question of the Hebrew poet, "What is man that thou art mindful of him?" Men in our day need to be encouraged to think of themselves as highly as they ought to think. They are waiting for some prophet of the Lord to say to them, one by one, "Son of man, stand upon thy feet."

It is an age of migrations, and many hearts are forlorn. Foreigners are coming to us by the millions, and our fellow-countrymen shift their residence with a frequency never known before in any land. Electricity and steam have converted us into a race of nomads. In this ceaseless movement of population there are gigantic perils. Breaking up the home often breaks up the foundations of morality. When men move in masses, the individual drops out of sight. Vast populations are pouring into the city to be swallowed up in the vortex of its boiling life. The man who stands out distinct in a village becomes invisible in a city. In the village his name is honored. He can speak to the richest banker, the leading merchant, even to the postmaster. But in the city he is quite ignored. His very existence is unknown. If he were in the penitentiary he would wear a number, but the city does not take the trouble even to give him a numbered tag. He could not escape from a prison without exciting commotion. He can drop out of city life without an eye winking. Cities are colossal destroyers of individuality. They are steam rollers, crushing men down into a common smoothness and flatness. Here is the preacher's opportunity.

Industrial forces are working ceaselessly to rob the individual of distinction. Machinery crowds men into factories and mills, where they are lumped together as so many "hands," pieces of an intricate mechanism turning out a commercial product. They are not quite animals, and not altogether full-grown men. Here is the preacher's opportunity.

Commercial forces are working to obliterate the individual. The small proprietor is disappearing.

Little business houses are swallowed up, and the man who once had his name painted above the door reappears with diminished stature as a manager of a section in a great department store, behind whose counters thousands of human creatures carry on a business for men whom most of them have never seen, and to whom they one and all are personally unknown. Business men are rolling themselves into corporations, syndicates, and trusts, each man disappearing deeper and deeper into the ever increasing bulk of the corporate body. It is a maxim now that corporations have no souls, so completely has the soul of the individual incorporator vanished from human sight. Here is the preacher's opportunity.

Even organized philanthropy has a tendency to lose the individual. Philanthropists interest themselves sometimes in sociological conditions simply as scientific phenomena. They study poverty, drunkenness, tuberculosis, as interesting social products. They publish volumes of statistics, giving a bird's-eye view of the dimensions of the vast ocean of want and woe, while manifesting no interest in any one broken family or any individual mangled life. Many good men are interested nowadays in the ocean, who have no disposition to look at the drops as they slip silently into the all-engulfing sea.   Here is the preacher's opportunity.

It is the lack of this personal touch which is multiplying our problems and deepening the blackness of the human tragedy.   One of the alarming facts of our world is the widespread absence of the sense of personal responsibility.   In the labor world outrages are often perpetrated which it is impossible to trace to the door of any ascertainable malefactor.   Men joined in a union sometimes do things which no one of them would think of doing if standing alone.   In the business world dishonorable and illegal operations are often carried on for which no one, apparently, is responsible.   Men merged in corporations seem to become capable of performing deeds to which no one of them if left to himself would ever stoop.   The sense of personal accountability decays when the distinctness of the individual fades.   To keep the lines of individuality vivid and sharp, this is the work of the preacher. "Where art thou?" and "Where is thy brother?" these are the first questions which a religious teacher is bound to ask, and he must ask them with such an accent that every man within reach shall know that they are addressed to him.   Personal responsibility both to God and to men is a theme for all times and places. If men lose sight of their own worth, they are sure to live unworthily. If they feel they are ciphers, they will not much concern themselves about their conduct. The moral lapses so common among immigrants in a new country are due largely to the decay of the sense of personal importance. In the old home they had a place which was recognized and a social significance widely acknowledged, but in the new land they are only insignificant drops in the human ocean, and what does it matter whether they cast back the sunlight from the crest of the billow or sink into the black ooze of the ocean bed? The demoralization of morals wrought by great cities is due to the crumbling of the sense of individual accountability. Thousands of men and women in all the world's cities have lost their grip upon the high things of life, because no one but God sees them. There is no one on earth who cares for their souls. Men are lost to the church as soon as they are submerged in the crowd. This is the preacher's opportunity. When other men are thinking and talking about classes and masses and races, it is more than ever incumbent on the ambassador of Christ to keep his eye on the individual man.

In fact the preacher is in danger of losing himself.

All the brooks have swollen into rivers, and all the rivers have widened into lakes and oceans. There is a sea of printed matter in which ministers are easily engulfed, a flood of administrative work by which they are frequently swamped, an ocean of questions and problems beneath whose troubled waters their pulpit usefulness oftentimes goes down. It is not hard for a minister to lose himself among ambitious speculations and utopian undertakings. Such words as "society," "humanity," "civilization," are enticing words to conjure with, and never has the temptation been greater than now to deal in spacious platitudes, unbounded generalizations, sweeping denunciations, and vaulting exhortations to nebulous duties whose contours are deeply buried in the mists. There are preachers who seem to be like Atlas, conscious that they are holding up the world. Unlike Atlas, however, their faces wear an anxious and despondent look. It would be better for them, and also for the cause of Christ, if they would roll the world from their shoulders upon the heart of God, and be content to carry simply the full weight of the responsibility for the spiritual development of the individual souls who make up their congregations.

The preacher needs the individual as truly as the

individual needs the preacher. Each human heart
is a page in the great book of life which the preacher
must learn to read. What can a minister know of
death until he shuts himself up in a room with a man
who is dying? How can he know anxiety at its
highest until he stands by the bedside of the little
invalid, and feels the heartbeats of a mother agoniz-
ing over the failing breath of her child? What can
he know of poverty until he enters the home of a
poor widow who is terrorized by the wolf at her
door? Remorse will be something real to him after
he has witnessed the agony of a conscience-tor-
mented man. He will preach better on the peace
that passes understanding after he has looked upon
a face in the hour of its spiritual transfiguration.
It is in the experience of the individual soul that the
preacher learns what this world is. The pathos of
life comes out in the sob of some one human spirit.
Human nature cannot be understood either in books
or in crowds. It is only when one heart is pressed
close against another heart, that heart secrets are
communicated. The preacher remains cold, and
his sermons are abstractions, until he folds his life
down round the lives of individual men. It is for
this reason that pastoral work is essential to the
highest preaching. Preachers who shirk pastoral

duty are always losers. They lose much themselves, and their churches lose still more. If orators, they may attract large audiences, but they do not do the work which is deepest and which lasts the longest.

It is because preachers do not come close enough to individuals that they sometimes form an unhuman style of speaking. To speak naturally ought to be the ambition of every preacher. He cannot afford to subtract from the force of his message by tones which repel or by intonations which offend. He ought to speak in the pulpit as a gentleman speaks when addressing his friends on matters of importance. If he uses tones never heard in the home, and cadences which would bring a laugh if used in any circle of society, he hurts the chances of his truth. The Christian pulpit has been a hotbed for the growth of all sorts of curious and unearthly tones. Twangs of various twists, singsongs of divers melodies, howls of different degrees of fury, and roars of many types of hideousness have tarnished the fame of the pulpit and caused the ungodly to blaspheme. The cause of these vocal monstrosities and outrages is that the preacher forgets he is talking to individual men. He thinks he is talking to the world, and that is why he shouts. He has the idea that he is preaching to the town, and consequently he roars. He imagines he is addressing a crowd, and his vocal mannerisms are caused by this foolish imagination. He gets his eye off the individual and his blunder reports itself at once in his elocution. The moment he comes out of the pulpit he speaks naturally. The most incorrigible pulpit howler or whiner speaks like a man as soon as he reaches the foot of the pulpit stairs. He is cured by remembering that he is talking to individuals. Let him remember this in the pulpit, and many of his elocutionary sins will fold their tents like the Arabs. Preachers do not preach to society or humanity or civilization. They preach to men like themselves. When they come face to face with the individual heart their style becomes natural, with every tone genuine and every inflection true. This is the cure also for diseases of rhetoric. There are stilts rhetorical as well as stilts elocutionary. A preacher who has imagination and a facile command of words is sure to go on rhetorical stilts unless he keeps his eye on the individual. The individual is the preacher's life-preserver. He is saved by him from unnaturalness. The natural style is the clear style. The first duty of a preacher is to make himself easily understood. He must keep in contact with his hearers all along the sermonic way.   To do this he must stand with both feet on the earth.   Most laymen cannot fly. If the preacher soars into the clouds, he goes alone. The clouds are a sorry place for a preacher.   The soaring preachers are not the preachers whom grown men like to listen to.   Juveniles of all ages sit awestruck, but the judicious grieve.   The Master stood ever on the ground.   His greatest sermons were earnest conversations.   He always spoke directly to the individual.   He says, "Follow me."

It is fidelity to the individual which insures a preacher's perennial freshness.   Many preachers become after a time intolerable, because of their monotony.   They lack variety both in the character of their subjects and in the manner of their treatment.   All their sermons seem to be prepared for an imaginary being whose age and sex and spiritual development never change.   Their congregation is to them simply a huge chunk of humanity, and to this living chunk they address their sermons.   But a preacher who wishes to escape monotony must mentally differentiate his congregation into groups, and then disintegrate these groups into individuals. Each group must receive its meat in due season. When Paul wrote to Titus in regard to his work among the people in Crete, he gave him an outline of the kind of teaching needed by the older men, another outline was suggested for the young men, still another for the aged women, another for the young women, and a different outline still for the servants. The temptations of age are not the temptations of youth, nor are the problems of men the problems of women. Masters need the emphasis at one point, servants at another. Paul recognizes these distinctions and would have each class instructed according to its capacities and needs. One cannot preach to everybody in general. There must be constant and keen-eyed discrimination. Truth must be cut into pieces according to the nature of those for whom it is intended. No one group in the congregation should be allowed to go hungry. Not one soul should be permitted to fall to the ground without the preacher's notice.

It is the individual who has much to do with keeping the preacher a Christian believer. The preacher who works for the reconstruction of individual men has no difficulty in believing in the reality and power of sin, nor is he likely to lose his faith in Christ as Saviour. It is when one grapples hand to hand with a man in the bondage of sin, that he realizes the limitations of legislation and the impotency of reformatory panaceas. He faces for the

H

first time the mystery of iniquity, and is not ashamed of the gospel, for he possesses demonstrative evidence that it is the power of God unto salvation to every one who believes. Men who nurse vague ambitions to lift the whole world frequently come to have foggy notions of the person of Christ. Losing one's grip on the incalculable value of a single soul seems to loosen one's grasp of the need of a personal Saviour. With the fading of the majesty of the individual the glory of the Divine Personality becomes dim. When the root trouble of the world is believed to be, not rebellion against God, but a faulty economic machinery, it is not easy to maintain a passionate devotion to him who was called Jesus, because he was to save his people from their sins. There are well-intentioned men who have much to say about the Christian consciousness, Christian principles, and Christian influences, who have allowed the personal Christ to fall into the background of their thinking. When men aim to reform society in general they are apt to trust to social forces and humanitarian influences, but when they strive to redeem one man only, they are compelled to cast themselves on the omnipotent God in Christ.

Work for the individual is essential not only for

the maintenance of faith, but for keeping bright the flame of hope. It is by finding one man that the preacher saves himself from despair. A crowd is always disconcerting, sometimes appalling. We are like Philip facing the five thousand whom he saw no way of feeding. It is only when we find in our congregation some one person — it may be only a lad — whose resources we can place in the hand of Christ, that light falls on the situation and the heart dares to entertain high expectations. To work for the bettering of the world as a whole is at the end of the day depressing. Changes are slow, steps of progress are infinitesimally small, the preacher is sure to die with the world apparently little better than it was in his boyhood. Unbelievers throw at him the taunting question, "Where is the fulfilment of the promise of his coming?" But the man who brings the gospel to individual hearts has always at hand a book of evidence more convincing than any written by the wise men of the schools. It is the faces of redeemed men in the pews that keep the preacher's heart singing through the disillusionments and discomfitures of a lifelong campaign. The transfiguration of a single life proves that Jesus is a living and a present power, and makes it easy to believe that every knee will some day bow to him.   The apostles faced with undaunted hearts angry and murderous Jerusalem because they could point to one jubilant man, and say, "By faith in His name hath his name made this man strong, whom ye behold and know." The preaching of Jesus was invincible, so long as one man kept crying, "Whereas I was blind, now I see." Preachers can work with patience and die in hope, if only they can see in the faces of men converted by their preaching the light of the glory of the knowledge of the blessed God.

The individual is also the nourisher of love.   One can love mankind in general, but it is a faint and feeble love, not the love that bursts into flame in sentences that burn their way into human hearts. It is when one heart touches another heart, that a fire is kindled which makes the whole church warm. There may be a growing interest in schemes and movements, with a progressive ossification of the heart.   Love is the one thing essential for the man who would preach the gospel, and love is fed and cleansed and glorified by repeated contacts with individual hearts and lives.

Let the preacher, then, seek and find the individual.   The glory of the temple is determined by the character of the material which is worked into it.

The stones must be hewn, shaped, and polished, and laid each one in its place with care. It is impossible to build a beautiful church out of unlovely material, to construct a glorious brotherhood out of unbrotherly Christians. Everything depends upon the character of the individual believer. The first thing to do is to separate him from his fellows and shut him in with God. Right relations must be established between him and the Eternal. The soul must feel its solitary relation to the Heavenly Father in order to realize to the full its obligations to the community. It is a high sense of individual responsibility to the Almighty, which is the basis of an enduring and fruitful altruism. Preaching must be clear at this point. The axe must be laid at the root of the tree. A man must be set right in his impulses and motives. He must be born again. It is easy to talk entertainingly of the sins of society and the prospects of humanity, but the critical business of the preacher is to put truth into the inward parts of the individual man.

The man, having started in the Christian life, must be trained to look upon himself as a builder. He is the fashioner of the temple of his soul, and the work of building must be carried onward through all the years. As Paul says, he is to pass from glory to glory, each succeeding character being more splendid than the character which went before it. As Peter says, he is to work diligently, "in faith supplying virtue, in virtue knowledge, in knowledge temperance, in temperance patience, in patience godliness, in godliness love of the brethren, and in love of the brethren love." Many church members do not grow in grace or in the knowledge of Christ because their minister does not instruct them. The spiritual life has its beginning, successive stages, processes, crises, temptations, perils, diseases, lapses, laws of growth; and in all these matters the preacher ought to be an expert. Many congregations wander about like sheep not having a shepherd, even though there is a man in the pulpit preaching sermons. He is interested in general truths and in the world as a whole, but does not understand the laws of spiritual development nor the kind of instruction by which the needs of the unfolding soul are satisfied.

Every follower of Jesus is to be made a positive force for righteousness in the church and community. To accomplish this, preaching must be constructive. Men must be told what they are to do, rather than what they are not to do. It is by learning to do well that they will cease to do evil. If they are trained to walk in the spirit, they will not fulfil the lusts of the flesh. Many publications rail constantly at evil-doing, and not a few ministers have caught this denunciatory spirit. But evil is most certainly overwhelmed, not by fixing the eyes on the things that are bad, but by turning the heart to the things that are good. If there be any virtue or any praise, these are the things worth expounding. Let the preacher deny himself the luxury of hurling thunderbolts, and give himself to the quiet work of building men in well-doing. It is better to work for the growth of one virtuous person, as Milton long ago pointed out, than to toil for the restraint of ten vicious persons. It is wiser to train one man to take an interest in things which are worth while, than to storm mangificently against practices and fashions which one would like to see abolished. This is to be remembered when you are tempted to preach a course of twenty sermons against present-day evils or popular amusements.

Christians are to be encouraged to develop the gift that is in them. Every soul is unique. For this reason the liberty of every individual is inexpressibly sacred. The rights of personality are never to be trespassed upon by the preacher. He must not expect all Christians to think alike, feel alike,

work alike. He must not demand that they all
shall be converted alike, pass through similar
emotional experiences, be equally confident of the
truthfulness of every phrase in the Christian creed.
It is not necessary that a church member shall think
and feel and work like the preacher or like the oldest
and saintliest of the church officials. The church
must be kept spacious. There must be room enough
in it for all temperaments and constitutions, all
grades of development, and all stages of culture.
There must be liberty for many schools of thought
and many types of service. To crush all Christians
into a common mould is a sin against the Christ
who wills that all men shall be free in him. The
preacher who considers those laymen who differ
from him as guilty of the sin against the Holy Spirit,
which hath no forgiveness either in this world or in
the world which is to come, is a man too narrow to
be intrusted with the guidance of men's spiritual
education. A preacher should rejoice if he preaches
to men and women who think for themselves, and
who have character sufficient to hold opinions different from his own. He should encourage every man
to be himself, shining with his own peculiar glory.
He should endeavor to throw round every member
of his church the influences which will call into

blossom the potential strengths and beauties which flow native in the blood. It is in the variety of moral graces, and in the diversity of spiritual attainments, that the church finds its richest life and becomes able to perform its widest service. Builders use materials of many shapes and textures in the construction of a cathedral.

Each member of the church is to be trained in the graces and obligations of brotherliness. He must be set at once in the midst of the brotherhood. You cannot put a man on a glass tripod and teach him brotherliness out of a book. He must learn brotherliness by being brotherly. He can be brotherly only when among brethren. To place each new convert in a circle of brothers, and to keep him there, is the work of the master preacher. A brotherhood cannot be built of men who are unbrotherly. One unbrotherly man in the circle of brothers works infinite confusion and mischief. Brotherliness is not a gift, but an attainment. It must be worked for through laborious years. It is not enough to have a brotherly intention, but the spirit must be disciplined and developed and trained. The obligations and duties of brotherliness must be learned and practised. The apostle who loved to think of the church as a temple also loved to think of each soul as a temple. The human personality is a shekinah. Every man is of value beyond computation. To build him foursquare in love is the work of the preacher. You are not a builder unless you build. Unless you build men you are a theorizer, a pedant, a declaimer. A doctor's business is not to know books, but to cure people. Your supreme business is not to build sermons, but to build characters. The preacher who does not count it a glorious privilege to build into the temple of God one particular pillar by whose splendid proportions and exquisite finish the glory of the entire temple shall be enhanced, is not in harmony with the heart of him who says, "Him that overcometh will I make a pillar in the temple of my God, and he shall go no more out; and I will write upon him the name of my God, and the name of the city of my God."

Peculiar attention to each and every particular part, this is the way of builders. A builder is a collectivist in his vision and an individualist in his method. Stone-masons to-day follow the fashion of the early Greeks in dressing one stone at a time. No matter what the size of the building, each stone receives definite and protracted attention. Our bricklayers follow the custom of the ancient Egyptians, and lay one brick at a time. No matter how many millions of bricks are to be laid, each brick is handled separately, for although the world is rich in inventions, no time-saving apparatus has thus far been devised to put out of use the traditional practice. The carpenter drives one nail at a time. He persists in this, no matter how large the contract or how pressed he is for time. The ingenuity of man has not created a device to supersede the time-honored procedure of driving nails one nail at a time. Surrounded by the miracle-working machinery of a new age, the builder clings doggedly to a policy which is old. Go to the builder, young preacher, consider his ways, and be wise.

It is the social aim of the builder which compels him to be an individualist in his method. A collectivist in vision, he is bound to be an individualist in practice. A building is an aggregate thing, and becomes possible only by a careful shaping of its constituent parts. It is the building as a whole which dictates to the builder what he is to do with each particular piece. Every part must be moulded with regard to every other part, for the parts must fit together in order to form the symmetrical whole. The nobler the edifice the more abundant the labor which is expended upon the individual stones. When a Parthenon is to be built, there is not a block of marble, however small, upon which genius will not do its perfect work.

The preacher is a builder, and like all builders he must see things in the large, and he must have an eye also for things which are small. He must gaze often at the finished temple, the glowing ideal let down from heaven, and he must study the possibilities of each and every living stone whose contribution of strength and beauty is to augment the splendor of the completed whole. The world is indeed the subject of redemption, but the world is to be redeemed one man at a time. Men cannot be made Christians in masses. That was the rock over which the Christian church first stumbled. It was in the days of Constantine that men first came into the church in crowds, and with the coming of the crowds began the early stages of a long eclipse. The cause of Christ has been indefinitely retarded because the church, eager to make haste, received men into her fold by tribes and baptized them by battalions. It is only when the church is willing to deal with one man at a time that the thrones of the kingdom of Satan are shaken, and that with the tread of a conquerer she strides toward the goal. Her vision must ever be social, but her method cannot be other than individualistic. It is her work to transform society; but society is made of individuals, and the character of the individuals fixes the character of society. It is her mission to elevate public opinion; but public opinion is simply the opinion of individuals, and the ruling opinion of a community is determined by the character of its citizens. Environment is a mighty factor in the moulding of life, but environment is after all made up of souls. Material surroundings are simply the creation of souls. In order to change the environment there must be a transformation of souls, and souls are re-created one at a time. The supreme work of the preacher is the changing of souls. If he turns aside to anything else, the service which humanity most needs is left unperformed. If the preacher is eager to alter the structure of the world, let him devote himself passionately to the work of bringing men one at a time to God in Christ.

This was the way of Peter. He began the work of social betterment by taking by the hand one of the many lame men in Jerusalem. The hand of one strong man clasping the hand of one man who could not walk is the frontispiece of the huge volume of church history. The beautiful deed at the beautiful gate teaches the lesson of Christian individualism. When Peter opened the door for the incoming

of the Gentile world, he opened it for one man —
Cornelius. Paganism in the mass did not present
itself as an applicant for baptism. Only individuals
were received to whom had been granted the gift of
the Holy Spirit.

This was Paul's way. It was not all Europe
which appealed to him in his dreams, but one solitary
and pleading suppliant. When he reached Philippi,
it was not to the city that he announced the good
tidings, but to a few humble women who had
not lost their faith in prayer. Paul found his way
into the heart of a new continent through the
heart of one woman — Lydia. His mission was to
admonish every man, to teach every man, that he
might present every man perfect in Christ Jesus.
It was worth while to pray and labor for one poor
runaway slave — Onesimus. Breaking the bondage
of one miserable demented girl was a triumph
never to be forgotten. The particularizing genius
of Paul reveals itself in all his letters. He had an
extraordinary eye for the individual. It was the
names of the men and women whom he personally
knew which made much of the music of his prayers,
and it was the memory of the particular persons
with whom he had labored and suffered and
triumphed that braced his heart in hours of loneli-

ness and peril, and opened up springs of gratitude and affection which flowed unceasingly. The man stands revealed in sentences such as these : " Salute Prisca and Aquila my fellow-workers in Christ Jesus ;" "Salute Epænetus my beloved ;" "Salute Mary who bestowed much labor on you; " "Salute Andronicus and Junias, my kinsmen and my fellow-prisoners."

This was the way of the Lord himself. He startled men by the piercing and particularizing glances of his eyes. "When sawest thou me ?" was a cry which burst from the lips of many. A woman supposed that she could hide herself in a crowd. A widow in the temple casting in her two mites did not dream that she was observed in the throng. He singled out a poor invalid at the pool of Bethesda whom no one had seen for nearly forty years. His heart was set on winning the classes, and so he paid assiduous attention to one man — Nicodemus. His soul yearned for the masses, and hence he gave himself to one degraded woman at the well. He longed to reach the uttermost part of the earth, and made the start by changing the heart of one man. It was the social vision that increased his zeal in working for the individual. It was because Jerusalem was on his heart that he was glad to brighten the life of one of her blind beggars. It was because he carried the world in his eye that he could see so clearly the strategic importance of the individual soul. The social order was iniquitous, and men begged him to strike it. He struck it by changing the spirit of a few peasants. The political order was corrupt, and men importuned him to overthrow it. He undermined it by raising the ideals of a few citizens. The economic system worked injustice and oppression, and men hated him because he did not overturn it with the point of his sword. He signed its death warrant by writing his name on the hearts of a few disciples. Outside of Palestine the nations lay moaning in the darkness. He saw them, and therefore steadfastly devoted himself to the building of twelve men. Of course the world called him narrow, foolish, crazy, devil-possessed; but he pursued his method to the end. His life's work seemed a failure. When he hung dying on the cross, Judea was as sordid, Samaria as lethargic, Galilee as worldly minded as when with radiant face he preached his first sermon in the synagogue at Nazareth. The Roman Empire was as cruel and the nations were as far from God when he cried upon the cross, "It is finished!" as when at his baptism he saw the heavens opened. But he did not die baffled or discouraged. "Be of good cheer, I have overcome the world." The world order was apparently unaltered, but here and there a human heart had caught his vision — the vision of a loving, sacrificing God, interested in each and every one of all his children, and with this his soul was satisfied. Just a few men aflame with the vision of God will change the atmosphere of society, and if you give them time, they and their successors will make new the structure of the world.

Christianity is the religion of the brotherhood. It is also the religion of the one man, the one man in and for the brotherhood. It is the religion of the one sheep, the one coin, the one boy. It is the religion which throws its arms around "one of these little ones," and which hears angels rejoicing over one sinner who repents. It is the religion which closets each man with God and which beholds each man alone at the judgment. It is the religion which pictures the Son of God standing on the doorstep, saying, "Behold I stand at the door and knock ; if any man hear my voice and open the door, I will come in to him, and will sup with him, and he with me."

This is God's way. He is the individualizing God. He is mindful of the one sparrow. The hairs of each human head are all numbered. We come

into the world one at a time.   Between the cradle
and the grave we each tread a path wide enough for
only one pair of feet.   We pass into eternity one by
one.   God delights in the work of shaping and guid-
ing the individual.   Science tells us that life began
upon our planet in jellylike, undifferentiated masses.
From the begininng, however, all the forces worked
unceasingly toward segregation and diversification,
until by and by the individual was set free.   With the
advent of the individual there began new wonders.
Within the individual the Lord of life added miracle
to miracle, until in a glorious moment human
personality emerged.   The personality was at first
rudimentary and inchoate, with all its endowments
embryonic.   In the early ages of human history the
individual is obliterated in the tribe, lost in the nation, merged in the life of institutions ; but through
the ages one increasing purpose runs, and the
individual man gradually increases in wisdom and
stature, until he at last steps forth in Christ the
sovereign of the world.   What is history but a long-
drawn drama in which the individual comes pain-
fully but irresistibly, and with the manifest favor
of God, to his own ?   Every form of collectivism
is doomed which does not develop the combined
energies and safeguard the total liberties and

rights of the individual man. Evolution has in many directions come to an end. The evolution of personality still goes forward. It does not yet appear what we shall be. We only know we shall be like him in whom and for whom we were created. His Father had been working for ages upon the individual man, and Jesus consecrated himself to the selfsame work. He began always with "a certain man." His word to us is, "Follow me !"

God is building human personalities. That is our work also. We are co-laborers with him. Great preaching is preaching which sets free the latent energies of the soul and builds up rich and potent personalities. All great preachers are alike in this, they create by their preaching resourceful, masterful, and Godlike men. The greatest gift which the church can give the world is a full-grown man, having in him the mind of Jesus. Measure your success as preachers not by the size of your congregation, which may after all be only a huge ecclesiastical jellyfish, drifting aimlessly and uselessly through the social sea, but by the stature and girth of the manhood which you develop in individual believers, by the brotherliness and serviceableness and Christlikeness of the separate disciples whom you build into the Christian brotherhood.

LECTURE IV

BUILDING MOODS AND TEMPERS

BUILDING MOODS AND TEMPERS

HAVING weighed the importance of viewing men separately, let us now look at them massed together. A Christian congregation is a human unit, and in a sense may be said to have a soul. Each member of the congregation contributes a separate character to form a composite character wonderful and unique. A power proceeds from each individual heart, and all these separate powers, when blended, constitute another and a higher form of power. A congregation of a thousand persons is something more than a thousand individuals. When men come together, certain latent forces are set free, and heightened capacities of thinking and feeling are unfolded in them. Where two or three are assembled, the Lord of Life is present in a way in which He is not present with the isolated soul. When two or three unite in prayer, heaven is responsive to degrees never reached when men pray separately. There are things to be done, therefore, with and for the church as a whole. A congregation possesses a disposition as pronounced and characteristic as that of any of its members.

This disposition must be moulded by the preacher. The moulding process passes through its most critical stages in the hours of public worship. The preacher is not simply an instructor, he is a fashioner of character, a maker of those moods and tempers which give character its bent and sinew. He is a builder, and his business is to construct a frame of mind.

He will do this in part by his sermons, and in part by other agencies ordained of God for the fostering of godly dispositions. Ideas have in them transforming power, and so also do certain attitudes and exercises. It is not the intellect only which is to be reached, but that great mass of instincts and sentiments which go to make up what we call the heart. Young preachers are always in danger of overestimating the intellect. Hungry themselves for ideas, and skilful in the art of playing with them, they not infrequently lose sight of those mighty, moving forces of the soul which lie deeper than all thought, and upon which religious leaders who would do enduring work must evermore rely. Genuine and living worship is something which every preacher covets for his church, but not every preacher gives himself devotedly to the work of opening the fountains from which the living streams

of worship flow.   If songs and prayers are not to
shrivel on the lips, there must be a rich interior
life, ministered unto according to laws which the
preacher ought to know.   Every preacher is desir-
ous that his people shall abound in good works, but
the impulse to work for God must be liberated
and strengthened, and this impulse has its home
and growth down in the deep places of the heart.
Many preachers accomplish little because they
do not go deep enough.   They cater to the intellect,
but do not stir the emotions.   They offer sacrifices
on the altar of logic and forsake the God-established
altar of sentiment.   They teach men the phrases of
an argument, but do not train them to sing a Te
Deum.   They labor to instruct them to understand,
but not to adore and wonder.   In one church the
minister is always preaching about work.   He goads
his people incessantly to action.   If men only are
doing something, life's problem is supposed to be
settled.   Themes for contemplation are steadily
ignored.   No attention is devoted to the deepening
of the channels of the emotions.   The inner springs
are quite forgotten.   Men are told what they ought
to do, but no attention is devoted to the creation of
those dispositions out of which fruitful activity
proceeds.   Such a church invariably grows thin.

People are worn out by the everlasting exhortation to be up and doing. The clank of machinery is always in their ears. The life of the church is a dusty plain. There is no mount of transfiguration. It is all street and no upper chamber. The souls of men are impoverished.

In another church the preacher is always explaining something. He has a philosophic mind, and delights in industrial entanglements, moral problems, doctrinal obscurities, and spiritual paradoxes. He speaks always to the intellect, and to that little corner of it which is interested in speculative puzzles. He leaves the heart out of account. He does nothing to stimulate or nourish the feelings. He shirks the work of building habits of humility, gratitude, and rejoicing. He does not know that men live by admiration, hope, and love. It is the heart which makes a preacher, and it is the heart which makes a church. The emotions give life its glow and glory. A starved heart means an enfeebled church. We have, then, these two classes of defective churches. In the first class, the church is an office in which various kinds of transactions are discussed and forwarded ; in the second class, it is a schoolroom in which divers doctrines and systems are unfolded and adorned. Blessed is the preacher who converts his church into a temple, and who, with or without pictured windows and without or with the help of ritual and rich architecture, creates by the conduct of the service an atmosphere in which souls instinctively look Godward. Atmosphere is everything.   If a church lacks atmosphere, we need not wonder that many will prefer to stay at home.   The church must give something which no other institution in the town can offer. There must be something in the sanctuary which the heart can instantly recognize as having come from upper worlds, and which will compel it to cry out : "This is none other than the house of God. This is the gate of heaven."   When a Christian man says he can get more help from books at home than from the service of public worship, it is because his nature is abnormal or because there is a fatal defect in the church service.   To build a worshipping mood in his congregation, to create an atmosphere in which souls shall stand awe-struck in the presence of their Creator, is a cardinal part of the preacher's stupendous task.

He cannot accomplish this without using all the agencies which the Holy Spirit has honored through the centuries.   To make the sermon the be-all and the end-all of public worship is a devastating blunder. Ministers who crowd praise and prayer into a corner, labelling them "preliminaries," do not know what they do. Among other things, they cut down the size of their possible congregation. The worshipping instinct is more deeply seated than is the sermon-hearing instinct, and more nearly universal. Many minds and hearts respond to the call to prayer which make no reply to the summons of a sermon. Little children drink in the music, and then fall asleep in the midst of the preacher's noblest argument. Plain and unlettered folk, lacking the intellectual discipline which enables them to follow the thread of a learned discourse, find relief and uplift in pouring out their hearts to God in song and prayer. Cultivated Christians, uninterested in the particular discussion or exhortation of the day, will go home edified if the service has been what it ought to be. Business men, fagged and jaded by the week's hard work, reluctant to grapple with a reasoned argument, are more likely to go to church if they are sure of finding there that which lifts and cleanses and furnishes them surcease of care. We preachers minister to a myriad-sided human nature, with manifold appetites and cravings, and the sermon is only one of many channels through which God's grace finds the soul.

Not only does the preacher increase the size of his congregation by ministering to men's devotional nature, but he expands its capacity for assimilating his message.   Preaching is a reciprocal business.   It is a matter of giving and taking, and the taking is no less important than the giving.   A sermon is a joint product, the creation of the preacher and the people.   The prosperity of a sermon depends both on the tongue that speaks and also on the ear that hears.   What matters it how consecrated and able the preacher, if the minds of the hearers are not prepared for his message ?   After the experiences of the week, men and women are in no mood on the Lord's day to listen without preparation to a spiritual message.   Confusions and distractions must be removed from the mind.   Alienations and resentments must be cleansed from the heart.   The stains of recent sin must be washed from the spirit.   Men have been laboring in separated fields, each one shut in by the bounds of his own specific task, and on the first day of the week they emerge from their isolation and all are together in one place.   Discordant feelings must be reduced to harmony.   Wandering thoughts must be subdued to reverent attention.   The sermon goes forth in vain unless the congregation is unified and hearts have become responsive and docile. Music and prayer are God's instruments for the taming of lawless impulses, and for the creation of spiritual unities and harmonies. A reverent mood is indispensable to the victory of a sermon. Reverence is the mother of attention, and men in their reverent moments listen gladly to truths whose home is in heavenly places. The more completely socialized the congregation, the more swiftly will the word of the Lord run and be glorified. He is an ignorant preacher who strives to make his sermon everything. By making it more than it can be, he makes it less than it might be.

To the preacher who desires the mightiest possible effect for his sermon, there are no preliminaries in the order of public worship. From the opening tone of the organ onward to the benediction, the service is a high and solemn transaction with God. The first thing essential in a Christian congregation is a reverential mood. The fear of the Lord is the beginning of wisdom, and without it a church service is empty and debilitating. To create and sustain this mood, the preacher must understand the value of silence and the indispensable influence of forms. It is for him so to plan as to secure those physical conditions which will enable the service to go forward unmarred and unimpeded. The worship must not be allowed to be trampled under the careless feet of late comers. Ushers must not flit up and down the aisles during the reading of the Scriptures or the singing of the anthem. Belated stragglers must not be granted a permit to proceed to their pews during the prayers. All late comers should be detained at the church door, and be permitted to take their seats only at stated pauses in the service provided for their accommodation. It is astonishing how careless many ministers are in the conduct of public worship. In ignorance or contempt of eternal spiritual laws, they allow the worship to degenerate into a slovenly and slipshod thing, devoid of all power to solemnize and elevate the heart.

Forms of worship are sacraments, visible signs of an invisible grace. There are ministers who seem to be afraid of them. Informality alone, so they think, is pleasing to the Almighty. To act in the house of God as one carries himself at home, and to speak to the High and Holy One who inhabits eternity, in the familiar, unconventional phrases of everyday life, is to them the only sure safeguard against formality and superstition. We do well indeed to be on our guard against formalism, for

formalism is the use of forms run to seed. But
forms are ordained of God. When rightly used,
they educate and bless. They are not only the
conservators, but the nourishers, of the life of the
heart. Without forms life cannot maintain itself
at high levels. It is by its forms that government
renders itself majestic, and society maintains its
tone. Religion is wedded to form by the will of
God. Posture in prayer is not a trifle. Behavior
in the house of God is a factor in the moulding
of character. The heart life is kept warm and true
by fine fidelity to the modes and patterns by which
it expresses itself. The forms of devotion in the
church should be kept dignified and beautiful.
Informality is not evidence of piety nor a scorn of
forms proof of exalted spirituality. It is fitting that
in the house of God worshippers shall show in their
outer conduct their sense of their sinfulness and
their consciousness of standing in the presence of an
infinite and holy God. In the making of moods,
forms are as essential as moulds are in the shaping
of bricks.

In the building of a reverential mood, no form of
worship is so efficacious as public prayer. It is
written that the apostolic church "continued steadfastly in the apostles' teaching and fellowship,

in the breaking of bread and the prayers." The men who were converted on the Day of Pentecost kept themselves alive by prayer. When the work of church administration began to absorb too much of the apostles' energy and time, they threw off this burden upon the shoulders of other men, declaring that it was their supreme business to give themselves to prayer and the ministry of the word. The preacher must always be a man of prayer. His spirit must be deeply devotional. If by nature he is not reverential, then by constant and arduous discipline he must bring his nature into subjection. He will give his days and nights to the study of the classics of the devotional literature of the church, and will meditate often upon the themes which have in them most power to solemnize and open the heart. Of Saul of Tarsus it was said, "Behold he prays!" This is the starting-point of all successful preaching. Only men constant in prayer preach the gospel with power. The preacher must lead his people in prayer. He must pray for them and with them. His prayers are in reality sermons. They are a part of his publication of the love of God. They are not picturesque and ceremonious preliminaries, moving in advance of his sermons, but are in themselves messages of his soul, opening up the way to

K

God.   All public prayer is of necessity seen of men,
and the form of it is consequently not to be despised
or slighted.   The form must be such as to help the
flow of the devotional feeling of the congregation.
Any feature of the prayer which rasps or jars, sub-
tracts from the power of the Holy Spirit in lifting
hearts to heavenly altitudes.   A preacher can shake
the entire fabric of a church's devotion by awkward
and ill-mannered praying.   Prayer is a form of
power, and the force of it can be broken by slipshod
sentences and rambling repetitions and effusive
clamorings.   The spirit of the prayer must of course
be right, but so also must its substance and form.
It is the duty, therefore, of the preacher to prepare
his prayers, — or at least to prepare for them, — and
no part of his work is more critical and taxing.
So immense is the labor involved that many men
shrink from it, either offering prayers entirely extempore, or entering a denomination which furnishes
the relief of a liturgy.   A man can read a prayer or
he can roll out offhand a string of prayer-shaped
sentences without spiritual preparedness; but to lead
a congregation week after week, year after year,
to the throne of grace along paths of the preacher's
own choosing lays a tax upon human nature to which
it is not easy to submit.   The man who uses a liturgy

is always tempted to rely upon the form rather than the spirit, and the man who throws away the liturgy is subjected to a temptation no less insidious and disastrous. Extemporaneous prayer is a form of liberty which harbors a multitude of sins. It is often taken for granted that because a man is given the privilege of framing each Sunday his own prayers he holds a license to mould them on the spur of the moment. The result is that in many a church there is a type of confused and deformed praying which is both scandalous and insufferable. Many a Christian of cultivation has been driven into a liturgical church, because he could endure no longer the unkempt and boorish prayers of his pastor. Men and women of refinement cannot be led to the throne of grace by a man who lacerates all the nerves of taste at every step in his supplications. Prayers as well as sermons must be prepared, not necessarily in every phrase and word, but by meditation and a careful survey, first of the needs of the congregation and then of the needs of the church universal. There was a superstition once that prepared sermons were an abomination to the Lord, inasmuch as that they interfered with the operation of the Holy Spirit upon the preacher's brain and heart in the hour when he stood before the people. Happily for the

world that superstition has passed away.   Experience has proved that the Holy Spirit has better
opportunity to work his will through a sermon
which has been prepared by long and patient labor,
than through the flighty and rhapsodical mouthings
of a preacher averse to study.   There is another
superstition from which the church is not yet quite
emancipated, the notion that a man can pray more
sincerely and more nearly in accordance with God's
will, if he trusts entirely to the guidance of the
Spirit as that guidance is offered at the passing
moment.   The two superstitions are alike.   Effective sermons cannot be, ordinarily, left to the caprice
or feeling of the moment, nor can a congregation be
most surely led to the throne of God by a man who
starts upon the journey not knowing by what route
he is going.   Stumbling here and there, retracing
one's steps now and then, using the wrong adjective
or adverb because the right one will not come,
these may be small matters to the Almighty, but
they are not small to men; and as the preacher is
praying for the sake of those who listen, he is bound
to use such verbal forms as shall best open men's
hearts for the incoming of God's spirit.

The content of prayer must also be carefully
considered.   Paul was particular, not only about

the spirit and manner of prayer, but also about the
petitions which should have a place in the worship
of the Christian society. He desired that the
prayers should have reach and range. They were
to include not only the men at the bottom, but also
the men at the top. Rulers and kings were not
to be forgotten, even though they had no sympathy
with the Christian faith. All sorts and conditions
of men were to be remembered, because it is God's
wish that all men shall be saved. The prayers in
the church were not to be folded round the local
congregation, or even the church universal; they
were to include the wide world. There was to be
a reach to the prayers, and a breadth, and depth.
The length and the breadth and the height were to
be equal. Not every preacher lives up to the
apostle's ideal. Public prayer often becomes con-
tracted in range, and is brought down to levels
lower than those on which the prayer of the church
ought to move. By carelessness in the shaping of
his prayers, a preacher may stunt not only his own
nature, but the spiritual sympathies and suscepti-
bilities of his people. If in his prayers he carries
on his heart the church universal and all nations
and races, his church will do likewise. More
things are wrought by the preacher's prayers than

the preacher himself dreams of. There have been ages in Christian history when the prayers drove out the sermon. There are churches in our age in which there is danger that the sermon may drive out the prayers. Both are ordained of God, and what God hath joined, let no preacher put asunder.

Music is also a form of power which may be used for the creation of those particular tempers in which the Christian religion finds delight. The gift of song is primeval. Man is by nature musical. By divine fiat he is a singing animal. Men have from the beginning loved music. There is a Lamech singing in the early dawn of the history of every people, and a Jubal fashioning harps and pipes. The Jewish church seized upon this natural aptitude and made use of it in the temple service, in every synagogue, and in every Jewish home. On the night on which Jesus was betrayed, he and his disciples, true to the traditions of their nation, sang psalms. Our Lord went into the shadows of Gethsemane singing. What the Jewish church did well, the Christian church has done still better. It was never known how much music lies in the human soul, till the angels sang their song of peace and good-will, and Jesus mellowed the hearts of men by his heavenly message. Music as we know it may be said to be the daughter of the Christian church. By liberating the heart, Christianity made a new development of music inevitable. When Pliny lifts the curtain and enables us to look upon a first century congregation in the act of worship, we behold it singing. The church of Christ has been singing ever since the Day of Pentecost. It is significant that with the coming of each new baptism of the Spirit there has come a fuller flood of song. The Lollards filled all England with their singing, and the followers of Luther struck terror into the Catholic hierarchy by their carols. The Wesleyans announced by their singing that a new epoch in Christian history had dawned. From the days of the apostles to the last church revival, it is true that when the Spirit of God moves mightily, the people burst into song.

This is because music is the language of the heart. Song is the natural speech of the emotions. When the heart is stirred, it sings. By singing it stirs itself still more deeply. Music not only expresses, but intensifies, the feelings. The mood which a song expresses is strengthened and perpetuated by the singing of the song. No man sings to himself. He sings also unto others. He communicates his mood to those who hear him. When men and

women sing together, they impart to one another
the sentiment of that which they sing, and thus
community of feeling is established, and spirits are
brought into beautiful accord.   If by prayer the
human heart is awed and elevated, then by song the
human heart is socialized and broadened.   Music
expands the sympathies and feeds the social nature.
Self-centredness and exclusiveness melt down under the reign of melody.   Touched by the spell
of harmonious tones, minds and hearts flow together, and the congregation becomes one soul.
Music is a language universal.   Every heart can
understand it.   Sentimentally every man is dis-
posed to music, even though organically he may be
like Charles Lamb, incapable of a tune.   In music
there is something heavenly before which earthly
moods and worldly tempers inevitably give way.
The basest man feels less sordid after he has been
immersed in a fountain of song.   The streams of
tone wipe out dividing lines, efface the springs of
bitterness, wear away estranging walls, and bring
the congregation out into a large and wealthy
place.   Music, when rightly used, does the very
work which the preacher wants accomplished.   It
develops the sense of fellowship and builds up the
brotherhood.

Like all things divine, music is dangerous. Many churches have what they call the music problem. Sometimes it is a music scandal. Many a preacher has heard the most heart-racking discords of his parish proceeding from the music. Music may convert itself into a peacock and exist only for the sake of display. Display in the house of God is abominable, and music when used for display, instead of being an angel to build up, becomes a devil to tear down. The preacher will therefore be watchful as to the personality and spirit of the man who is chosen leader of the church music. The musical director must be a Christian man. He is an appointed minister of Christ, and must therefore have the spirit of Christ. The man who leads the service in which emotion is predominant and the man who leads the service in which thought is regnant have equal need of the baptism which comes from heaven. A church should no more think of placing its music in the hands of an unchristian man than of inviting to the pulpit a man making no professions of Christian discipleship. How can a pagan and a Christian work together in Christ's temple? More than one church has been unaccountably blind at this point, and has paid more than double for its unpardonable blunder.

With the musical direction in the hands of a Christian man, large latitude may be allowed in the selection of musical forms. There is no reason why a part of the musical service should not be led by one voice, or by two voices, or by three or four or eight voices, or by a chorus of a large number of voices. One voice can do what many voices cannot do, and a quartette can do things which are impossible to a soloist or a chorus. In the interpretation of the musical masterpieces of adoration and thanksgiving, there are diversities of ministrations, and the same Lord; and diversities of workings, but the same God who worketh all things in all. The one thing to insist on is that the people shall be granted their rightful place in the worship. All the people must be given opportunity to sing. The entire company of the redeemed must utter praises. Worship must not be monopolized by a class. All Christians are priests unto God. To silence the congregation is to quench the Spirit. If the church prefers to remain dumb, it is because its life is at low ebb. A silent church must be trained to become vocal. Only a songful church can listen appreciatively to a sermon or engage triumphantly in Christian service. If the people sing badly, the next step is not to clip the hymns and lengthen the sermon, but to make room for additional hymns. If a church does not like to sing, it is because it is emotionally depleted. New life can be imparted, not by increased intellectuality in the pulpit, but by a freer exercise of the heart in the pews. When Paul exhorts Christians to awake from their sleep and to arise from the dead, he bids them to speak one to another in psalms and hymns and spiritual songs, making melody with their hearts to the Lord, giving thanks alway for all things in the name of the Lord Jesus Christ to God. Singing is not then a preliminary of the sermon, something to be indulged in until the late comers have arrived, or an interloper to be watched constantly with a jealous eye, but a sort of preaching, a public proclamation of the goodness and longsuffering kindness of God. It is a means of grace and helps one to say, "I believe in the communion of saints." The preacher who wishes to bring his church into the attitude and disposition of Christ, and to fortify it against unchristian tempers, will steadily make use of the tongues of his people in the musical exercises of praise. Many a minister would to-day have a larger and more responsive congregation, had he only persistently and systematically encouraged his people to take part in the service of song.

Bible reading is another agency ordained by God for the creation and upbuilding of moods. Like prayer and song, it is also a form of preaching. It antedates our modern sermon. Through centuries of Jewish history the reading of the scriptures was the chief source of instruction and inspiration to the people. At the council of Jerusalem, James identified preaching and reading when he said, "Moses from generations of old hath in every city them that preach him, being read in the synagogue every Sabbath." Why should we not regard the public reading of holy scripture as a form of preaching, not a preliminary to be hurried through while the members of the congregation are finding their pews, but an integral and cardinal part of the preaching service? It is strange indeed that any man who believes in the unique inspiration of the men who wrote the Scriptures should be willing to read the Bible with lukewarm and begrudging emphasis, putting his own words in the place of honor, and using the sentences of prophets and apostles and the Lord himself as humble avenues leading up to the splendid palace of his own august creation. If it be true that God of old time spoke in the prophets by divers portions and in divers manners, and that at the end of those days spoke to us in his Son, it is certainly unbecoming in preachers to read the Scriptures with conspicuous negligence or hurry through them as though they were a barrier shutting men out from the rich pastures of the sermon. And if it be a fact, as Paul declares, that "every Scripture inspired of God is also profitable for teaching, for reproof, for correction, for instruction which is in righteousness, that the man of God may be complete, furnished completely unto every good work," it would seem that the preacher has no more important duty than reading these Scriptures to his people.

There are reasons why Bible reading in the church should just now be exalted. We are living in a hurried age, and the pressure of life is tremendous. Men are driven through the days and weeks as by so many furies, and because of this precipitate haste, certain customs which flourished in the former times are falling into desuetude. Family worship is not so common in Christian homes as it was a generation ago, and the Bible has been supplanted in many circles by the magazines and papers. Let the preacher read the Bible to a generation too preoccupied to read it for itself. During the entire lifetime of men now living, the Bible has been the subject of vehement and distracting controversy.

The old theories of inspiration and inerrancy have been found untenable, and a new conception has not yet been completely formed in the popular mind and heart. Laymen in large numbers are bewildered by the swarms of critical theories as to the origin and authority of the Bible, and from this bewilderment many preachers themselves have not emerged. The movement of Biblical criticism was inevitable. It is not to be lamented, but rejoiced over. Scores of conscientious scholars have labored with enthusiasm and fidelity to ascertain the facts in regard to authorship, and the formation of the canon. Results have been obtained, numerous, substantial, and invaluable. But in all such movements there is much human frailty and imperfection. Theories are often advanced with nothing to commend them but their novelty, and conclusions are promulgated upon which it is unsafe to build. A considerable part of all that has been published in the name of higher criticism is hay and wood and stubble, and will be some day viewed with the same amused wonder with which we now look at the dreary speculations of the schoolmen. Critical theories, proclaimed with blast of trumpets and received with a shout, fall dead one after the other, and no matter what the present dominant theory is, the chances are that the feet of those who buried its predecessor are at the door ready to carry it out. Every thinking man must of necessity have a theory of the Bible, but it is important to remember that the Bible is more than any theory of the Bible. Young preachers filled with the latest speculations of the schools sometimes err in making their notions of the Scriptures more conspicuous than the Scriptures themselves. It is possible so to overlay the Bible with hypotheses and guesses as to prevent it doing its God-appointed work. No matter what your view may be of the composition and structure of the Scriptures, read them to your people. The last word of Biblical criticism has not been written. Many of the conclusions of the latest scholarship are only tentative and will be revised several times before your heads are gray. Read the Bible to your people without comment. Do not muffle its music in the folds of your conjectures. Let its organ tones sound out, finding those who have ears to hear. Do not dim its light by your assumptions. Let it shine undarkened by interpretations. Do not quench its fire by your suppositions. Let it radiate its heat, and who knows how many hearts may be melted. Do not dull the edge of it by wrapping round it your conceits or guesses. Let it cut. It may prove to be even in the twentieth century "living and active and sharper than any two-edged sword, and piercing even to the dividing of the soul and spirit."

No matter what you may think of the Pentateuchal sources, or of the number of Isaiahs, or the authorship of the Psalms, or the extent of interpolated passages in the Gospels, the fact remains that the Bible is the book of books, and is able to make wise unto salvation through faith which is in Christ Jesus. It is a world power, and the wise preacher will make generous use of it.   He can build up his congregation by reading the Scriptures.   Men who care little for his sermons will come to church if he knows how to read the prophets and apostles.   His congregation will grow constantly in sensitiveness to religious appeal and in capacity for assimilating religious truth, if only it is steeped in the Scriptures.   The more of the Bible men hear, the more will they want to hear.   It is not because people know the Bible that they take scant interest in sermons.   It is because they are ignorant of it.   It is the children who have been fed the Scriptures from infancy who become the men and the women who listen with keenest appreciation to what the preacher has to say. The lad in Lystra who was most attracted by the travelling preacher, Paul, was the boy who knew from a babe the sacred writings. If you desire a congregation hungry for your sermons, then read them the Bible. It contains the food which builds up the faculties to which a preacher speaks, and upon which he must rely. It is a book of voices, thrilling, piercing, mysterious voices whose accents stir powers in the human soul which are deep and sleeping and haunt the spirit with a bewitching music which will not let it go. It finds men both at their highest and their deepest. It sweeps through a wider gamut of thought and feeling than any one man is master of. It offers a more myriad-sided wisdom than any one soul possesses. It will reach men whom you in your sermons will never reach. It creates moods and chastens tempers as no other book in all the world. It produces a climate in which sermons come to luxuriant growth. For your own sake you need to read the Scriptures to your people with mind and heart and soul. It is when a man is filled with the spirit which burned in the hearts of the Bible saints and heroes that he feels most like preaching. It is then that he cries, "Woe is me if I do not preach." The Bible builds up both the laity and the clergy. Its words are spirit, they are life. They stir and kindle, they illumine and move. They have hands and feet, they

L

work miracles. Men who drink them in become able to stop the mouths of lions and to quench the violence of fire.

Prepare yourselves, therefore, to become Bible readers. Train yourself with that end in view. Discipline your voice until it becomes flexible and capacious, capable of expressing the emotions which the prophets felt, and the visions which the apostles saw. Practise Bible reading every week. Perfection comes only by practice. The art of reading is a fine and difficult art, and no man learns in his sleep how, by modulation and by accent, by intonation and by emphasis, to interpret the sentences which have been written for men's comfort. There is no excuse for shabby Bible reading. Not every man can be a brilliant preacher, but every man can be a good Bible reader. If he cannot himself create great sermons, he can read with grace and force the sermons which holy men of old delivered. Let us hope the time will come when no man will be graduated from a theological seminary without having passed an examination in Bible reading, and when no man can be ordained to the Christian ministry who is not a good Bible reader. Negligence at this point is not only mental dullness but a moral delinquency.

Resolve, then, to read the Bible generously to your people. Read the Old Testament as well as the New, the Epistles no less than the Gospels. Do not allow your people to infer that there are only a few narrow shreds and isolated patches worthy of a modern man's attention. Keep alive in men's hearts reverence for the Bible as a whole. Read its history and poetry, its biography and letters, its sermons and its prophecies. Read them in all the meetings of the church, in the meetings of public worship and in the prayer meeting, in the Bible school and in the missionary societies. Drench your church in the spirit of the Bible. Read it like a man of prayer. Read it like a prophet of Jehovah. Read it like a lover subdued by its message. New light will break forth from it every time you take its words upon your lips. God has spoken often through the book, and often will He speak again. Great preachers live on the Bible. Their supreme delight is giving the Bible to the people. Essayists, lecturers, and clerical adventurers of divers types may make a stir for a season in the Christian pulpit, but the ages are not deceived. The church, on looking backward and counting up her pulpit princes, admits no one to the shining company of the immortals save those alone who have been mighty in the Scriptures.

The work begun and developed by Bible reading, praise, and prayer is carried on and perfected by the sermon. The church of Jesus must be reverent, grateful, sympathetic, hospitable, jubilant, and loving; and to make it this is the preacher's occupation. In the growing of moods, we do well to remember that nothing in God's universe takes place by chance. The preacher, like the farmer, works under a God of law, and the same obedience and industry which bring forth corn and potatoes will no less certainly secure the fruits of the Spirit. The flowers of paradise like all other flowers are within the reach of all who are willing to expend the necessary labor. Heavenly plants, as well as plants of the earth, must be watered and cultivated. If a church is not beautiful and fragrant it is largely because the spiritual gardeners have been ignorant or lazy. It is for them to create the climatic conditions under which celestial seeds come to blossom and fruitage. There is no reason why the word of the preacher should year after year return to him void.

Moods, then, are the preacher's first concern. His earliest work is to bring his people into a Christian frame of mind. What men are willing to believe depends largely upon their mental mood. A preacher forgets this at his peril. Let him beware how he tries to introduce new interpretations and doctrines into a church whose mind is inhospitable. Some churches are in a shell. The new preacher sees this at a glance. He proceeds forthwith to drive into it a series of logical and pointed discourses on the particular doctrine upon which the church in his judgment needs enlightenment, whereas he ought first by the patient exposition of old truths in which every one believes create an atmosphere under whose genial influence the shell will open of itself. Men cannot be driven into believing things by argumentative sermons, but are made hospitable to new truths by the gradual transforming of their minds. It is not by mental force or brilliant argument that inadequate or erroneous conceptions are gotten rid of, but by elevating the whole plane of thinking and raising the temperature of the life of the heart. A church will believe what it ought to believe only when it is in the right mood.

If the preacher desires to create a sympathetic and social temper, he will pay attention to his vocabulary. He will eschew so far as possible all technical and abstract words. Words which are cold and unfamiliar will be promptly banished and only those retained which the heart knows. Words used by specialists and words born in dis-

tant lands will give place to the native words which
are used in street and school and home. To come
close to men the preacher must speak to them
in the language in which they were born. It is the
words of the mother tongue which find the blood.
There is a necromancy in language and a preacher
ought to understand and use its magic. Words
in themselves are powers and have strange potencies
to awaken desires, quicken impulses, create ambitions, give shape to ideals and direction to feelings,
and kindle all those subtle flames which burn upon
the soul's central altars. Some preachers use a
vocabulary cold enough to form icicles. Their sermons sound like pages torn from an almanac, or a
text-book, or a volume of statistics. They are not
acquainted with the words which poets use nor
can they speak the syllables which start and feed a
fire. Words have moods as people do, and the
preacher must be master of the words which carry in
their hearts the dispositions which he desires to communicate to his people. There are reverent, kneel-
ing words, warm, tender and affectionate words,
open-handed, open-hearted, hospitable words, laugh-
ing, shouting, hallelujah words — words which are so
rich in human experience, so saturated with laughter
and tears, that if the preacher breaks them upon his

congregation they fill with perfume, like precious
alabaster boxes, all the place where he is preaching.

Even more careful will he be of his themes. He
will never remain away long from the great subjects.
If men are to feel deeply and enlarge the organs of emotion, they must have something great to think about.
Exhortations to enthusiasm and other emotions are
sounding brass. Feelings come, not by the cudgel-
ing of the will, but by the contemplation of facts and
truths which pierce and expand the heart. Mighty
moods are created only by majestic visions. Let the
preacher, therefore, avoid thin issues, petty questions,
trifling topics, and devote himself to the sovereign
features of the revelation of God in Christ, and to
those imperial interests which concern the universal
heart. He will not make his sermons chambers of
horrors, dealing constantly with the world's outrages
and scandals, but he will on the Lord's day unveil
the face of the One who is the fairest of ten thousand, the One altogether lovely. The mind that was
in Jesus is the mind which the preacher is to build up
in his people, and it is by looking again and again at
the Man of men that the soul passes from glory to
glory, being changed into his own image. To produce the Christian mood there is no method equal
to that of Paul, preaching Jesus and him crucified.

But fully as important as his theme is the spirit
and manner of the preacher. Moods are conta-
gious. "Like priest, like people." There are narrow
and crabbed congregations made such by a bigoted and surly curmudgeon in the pulpit. Some
churches are hard and intolerant because of the pig-
headed dogmatism of the preacher. Parishes are
sometimes cynical and misanthropic because a
clerical Thersites stands at the centre. There are
congregations which are irreverent and simpering
because of the jaunty worldling who officiates in holy
things. Many a church is glum and discouraged
because its pastor is lachrymose and drooping. As
soon as a preacher finds himself pitching all his
sermons in a minor key, he ought to resign or be
granted a vacation. Preachers are ordained to build
up in men the mood of faith, not of doubt; of hope,
not of despair; of love, not of denunciation and
fault-finding. Joy is one of the surest evidences of
the presence of the Lord. A dejected or despondent
church has lost the note which made the apostolic
church invincible. The Christian pulpit lies in
the gleam of a triumphant spirit. In all true Christian preaching the trumpets are sounding all the
way. The cross is evermore in sight, and so also is
he who said and says: "Be of good cheer, I have

overcome." The preacher must, by word and life, teach his church the art of always rejoicing. We live in a world of gigantic wrongs and heart-rending tragedies. The fires of hell are burning at our doors. Strong men will sometimes flame and thunder, and weak men will often sob and whimper; but Christian preachers are sent from God, not simply to hurl thunderbolts at the world's demons and dragons, or to paint with lurid rhetoric society's cancers and abominations, but rather to inspire the heart with sentiments which will by and by put an end to ancient slaveries and create a soul under the ribs of death.

It is not for every preacher to be pastor of a large church, but every preacher may covet the joy of shepherding a church beautiful. If men judge a church by the size of its membership, God judges it, we may be certain, by the height of its ideals, the range of its sympathies, the reach of its aspirations, the depth of its convictions, the fineness of its temper, the graciousness of its disposition, and the wealth of those graces which he saw in his well-beloved Son. When you find you cannot increase the size of your church, go to work with fresh energy to increase the dimensions of its soul. Quality of life, and not quantity, is what counts most in working out God's plans. The church of Christ must first of all be beautiful. She represents the wooing, winsome Jesus, and she conquers only by her grace. Her mind must be sympathetic, her spirit gracious, her touch gentle, her face radiant, and her temper sweet. She must be disciplined to walk in the ways the Master loves. She must have his simplicity and tranquillity, his poise and indescribable charm. She subdues, not by driving, but by the irresistible fascination of her loveliness. It is by transforming, with God's help, the mood of the church that we preachers are to change the face of the world. The church is a medium of revelation, and it is only when it incarnates the disposition of Jesus, that the nations will behold in it the manifold wisdom of God.

LECTURE V

BUILDING THRONES

BUILDING THRONES

In the world's speech, "throne" is the symbol of power. By the building of thrones is meant in this lecture the generation and development of moral forces, the creation and organizing of spiritual potencies. The New Testament pictures the Founder of the Christian religion as a man of might. He is a miracle worker and a fountain of new forces. Streams of energy flow from him. Nature and humanity are alike responsive to his touch. People stand astounded at the things which he does. Wherever he goes he stirs the crowds mightily, and men confess that they have never seen it after that fashion. He places himself upon a throne, and the New Testament writers leave him there. All authority is given unto him. He is King of kings and Lord of lords.

"Ye shall sit on thrones," so he said to the men who were nearest to him, and when he sent them out he gave them power to tread upon things that hurt. His parting promise to them was a fresh baptism of strength. "Ye shall receive power" — so he said as the cloud covered him. What he said to the Twelve he says to all. The climax of his promises to the churches is, "He that overcometh will I give to him to sit down with me in my throne."

The preacher, then, is a servant of a King, and his message is a form of power. Such was the conception of the first great preacher. "I am not ashamed of the gospel, for it is the power of God unto salvation to every one who believes." The man who carries the message thus becomes a man of power. An impotent preacher is no preacher at all. Preachers are to be ranked by what they accomplish. They are not to be measured by their learning, or language, or elocution, or reputation, but by what they achieve. Only he is a great preacher who brings great things to pass. Sermons are nothing unless they are social forces. If they do not work, they are clanging cymbals. It is expected of a minister that he shall be influential, that an energy shall flow from him into the lives of men.

Since every man has immediate access to the heart of God, and is privileged to share in the divine grace, every regenerated soul becomes a centre from which celestial energy is radiated. On the day of Pentecost there was a light on every forehead, a song in every heart. All were participators in the overmastering power from heaven. Under the new dispensation every believer sits on a throne, and influences go out from him over a kingdom whose boundaries are known only to the Lord. The faith was delivered to the saints, and so also were the keys. The power of binding and loosing does not belong to clergymen alone, but is in the hands of the society of believers. Ideally, every Christian is a prophet, a priest, and a king. In Christ, God calls us one and all to sit enthroned.

The church, then, is a form of power, a huge complex of blended energies, created for the purpose of working upon the world's thought and conduct. The church universal is the one supreme world power for moulding ideals and re-creating dispositions. To make it increasingly regnant in society's business and bosom is the work to which preachers are called.

All this is written large across the pages of the Scriptures. Abraham believed that through him all the families of the earth were to be blessed. Isaiah saw a light going forth from Jerusalem illumining the isles of the sea. The church does not exist for itself. It is a steward of the divine bounty. Its treasures are all held in trust. It is elected, not for the enjoyment of favors, but for service. It lives and labors for humanity. "For their sakes, I sanctify myself," these are the Master's words, and the church, when true to him, makes them her own. The road to greatness lies through service, and the true church is the church which says, "I am among you as one who serves." When Jesus sent out the Twelve, they were given power to heal as well as to preach, to cast out demons as well as to teach. His favorite figures all carry in them this idea of going forth with power to serve. "Ye are the light of the world." Light does not exist for itself, but for the eyes of those who sit in darkness. "Ye are the salt of the earth." Salt does not exist for itself, but for that which it saves from putrefaction. "Ye are the leaven." Leaven does not exist for itself, but for the bread which it renders palatable and nutritious. Light and salt and yeast are enthusiastic and indefatigable workers. "Go!" was Jesus' constant exhortation, and round his youthful church he wrapped on the day of his ascension this great commission — "Go, disciple the nations!" The church, as Jesus saw it, was not a Noah's ark in which a favored few were to be carried through the flood, but rather a brotherhood of workers, pledged to God and to one another for the cleansing of society and the getting of Heaven's will done upon this earth. If the church hides its life under an ecclesiastical bushel, the members of the world's household will remain in darkness. If the church is not useful, it is like salt which has lost its savor, good for nothing but to be cast under foot of men. If it does not make itself felt in the community, it fails to represent the living, mighty God. If it does not lay down its life daily for the good of men, it does not follow in the footsteps of its Lord. It is true to its Founder only when it is a society of saviours, an instrument of social redemption, an angel troubling the waters of the pool in which humanity is to be healed. Its work lies in Jerusalem, and also in Judea, and also in Samaria, and also in the nations which lie in the darkness on the outer edge of the world. It is a planetary power.

The New Testament church is a working, self-sacrificing, conquering society of brothers; and this is the church which the world to-day is calling for with a passionate insistence which cannot go unheeded. The ages in which the church stood dreamy and idle, waiting for a new heaven and a new earth, have gone, never to return. The idea of the church as a city of refuge, into which sinners may flee for the saving of their souls, is no longer tenable among thoughtful men. "Come out from among them, and be ye separate," can no longer receive the monastic inter-

M

pretation. Individual redemption is the starting-point, but world redemption is the goal. Religion is more than a personal possession of security and peace and joy, it is a service, a sacrifice, a gift to others. Men are praying "Thy kingdom come" with a new passion. Religion is now seen to concern this world no less than the world which is to come. The good things which have been promised are not all to be waited for until we put on immortality. We have a right to hope, not simply for the rescue of a few of the ship's passengers, but for the saving of the entire ship. The kingdoms of this world are not hopelessly in the hands of the devil, but will become, when Christian consecration and sacrifice have done their work, the kingdoms of our Lord and his Christ. This transfer of emphasis from the other world to this is one of the mightiest of all the changes which have been wrought in Christian thinking within the last hundred years, and it brings to the front for fresh discussion the question, What is the mission of the church? Men are asking to-day with irritating intensity and repetitiousness: "What is the church doing? What mighty works does she perform to-day? What evil spirits is she casting out? What diseases of society is she healing? Where are the serpents and the scorpions which she is crushing?"

The old-time stress on creeds has been shifted. The first question now is not, What do you believe? but, What are you doing to make a better world? The old inquiries as to emotional experiences have been superseded by queries in regard to good works. The one parable of Jesus with which the twentieth century is most familiar is the parable of the good Samaritan, and the words of the New Testament which can be seen the farthest, and which are read by the largest number of living men, are the closing words of that same parable — "Go and do thou likewise." It is a humanitarian age. The only religion which appeals to thousands is a religion which exalts and glorifies service. You may quarrel with this mood if you will, and say that it is running to extremes, but you are not likely to suppress it. A new spirit is abroad and its voice is heard throughout the world. Men are laying an emphasis on social problems and the social applications of religion, which is quite unique in Christian history. No doubt this is the Lord's doing, one of the signs of the times which only blind men will fail to note and ponder. It is always well to meet men where they are, for it is only as we are willing to meet them there, that we have any chance of leading them where we think they ought to be. If you take scant interest in the practical aspects of religion, and show ignorance of the social and industrial movements of your time, you will alienate many of the noblest spirits in your congregation. If you do not give your people tasks to do, and lead them into spacious fields of practical endeavor, you must not be surprised when they wander off by twos and threes, as they surely will, and attach themselves to congregations which are doers of the word and not hearers only. We live in the midst of a restless, energetic people, a people not over fond of definitions and abstract thought, and the only way to escape disaster is to cut generous channels through which this tumultuous energy can flow. The generation of moral power and the application of it, this is the fascinating problem to which the preacher will again and again return.

It is the complaint of many ministers that their people will not work, but the fault does not always lie with the people. It may be that the minister does not know how so to strike the rock of the human heart as to cause the streams of force to flow without which effective action is impossible. The hearts of men must be cultivated with all diligence, for out of the heart are the moving forces of the world. Conscience is a power, and so are sympathy, affection, good-will, enthusiasm, loyalty, devotion, aspiration;

and the preacher must preach in such a way as to increase the stock of each and all of these. He ought to ask himself unceasingly: "How can I give a new edge to conscience and a new height to aspiration? How can I arouse the social sympathies and sentiments? How can I create the moral enthusiasm and spiritual passion without which society must degenerate and shrivel? How can I increase the capacity of the church dynamo for creating the moral forces by which all the wheels of philanthropy and social betterment throughout the town shall be kept turning? How can I replenish the spiritual forces of humanity, that the material development of the community may not outstrip its moral growth?" The man who faces questions such as these will not preach narrow or stupefying sermons. He will cultivate in his people the habit of looking outward. He will cut windows in his discourses opening out upon the public square. He will keep the church doors ajar, and preach a gospel which carries the world's horizon in its eye. It is when the preacher has no vision that the people become sluggish and perish.

There are preachers who do not know how to use their people even after they are aroused. They do everything themselves. Soon or late they become

jaded and discouraged and begin to say damnatory
things about the selfishness and laziness of church
members. In many cases the discouragement is
due to the preacher's own ignorance and folly.
He made himself the one and only parish dynamo.
He did not roll the burden of parochial work upon
the shoulders which God had provided to receive it.
He allowed his people to think of themselves as a
select society to be ministered unto, when it was his
business to train them to minister and to give their
lives a ransom for others. A minister should use
his people. He need not carry them. They are
able to walk. The farther they walk the better.
He need not do their work. The more they work
the more do they grow in grace and in the knowledge of Jesus Christ their Saviour. To do their
work for them is to blast their spiritual development and lay upon their substitute a burden too
great for flesh and blood to bear. Even Moses
tottered under so heavy a load. "I am not able to
bear all this people alone, because it is too heavy
for me. Kill me, I pray thee, out of hand, and let
me not see my wretchedness." And the reply of the
Almighty was, "Gather unto me seventy men of the
elders of Israel and I will take of the spirit which
is upon thee and will put it upon them; and they

shall bear the burden of the people with thee, that thou bear it not thyself alone." This was the method of Jesus. He did not attempt to redeem Palestine unassisted. He rolled the great enterprise upon twelve men, and then upon seventy, and then upon one hundred and twenty. The apostles would not allow themselves to be crushed by getting under all the work which the church found to do. They called out the resources of men whom God had raised up for their assistance. If it be true that the spirit of God has come upon all classes, the old and the young, the women as well as the men, why should the minister not make use of his entire church membership in getting done the things which ought to be accomplished?

There are ministers who do not know how to organize their people, and then censure them for working ineffectively. To build the principle of co-operation into the life of the church is to augment its power enormously. Capitalists have learned how to organize money, and it is by consolidated gold that they are working their miracles. Industry has mastered the art of combination, and a new era has dawned for labor. It is for ministers to organize character, to marshal conscience, to coördinate and link together moral forces in such ways as to hasten the coming of the golden age. If one can chase a thousand, and two can put ten thousand to flight, what may be expected when a hundred or five hundred Christians are amalgamated into a compact body, inflamed by the spirit of the Lord, and led by a man who knows how to blow from a bugle a blast which is not uncertain?

It is only by patient drilling that armies are prepared for battle, and it is only by long-continued training that Christians are fitted for effective service. Telling church members that they ought to work is not enough. Some preachers have a gift for exhortation, and after that there is no more which they can do. They exalt the glory of performance and urge the necessity of laboring for God, but they never point out the specific tasks which it is possible for their people to work at. Or if they name the task which is to be attempted, they do not designate the successive steps which must be taken in order to reach the goal. Laymen need leadership in the realm of Christian effort, no less than in the region of Christian thought. It is as easy to overestimate men's knowledge of how to work as it is to underestimate their willingness and ability to work if only properly instructed. A large proportion of church members are novices in Christian service, and must be led on from point to point, like children in a kindergarten, with infinite patience and particularity of instruction. Work must be broken into bits, and the bits distributed to groups and individuals, with detailed suggestions as to the best way of doing it. Working for the redemption of a community is a fine art, and all of us are bunglers at first, gaining proficiency only after many pains and botchings. The gift of encouragement is more valuable than the gift of exhortation, and the pastor who encourages his people to take hold of certain definite tasks, and heartens them step by step as they proceed along the way, will bring to pass achievements forever beyond the vehement exhorter who is everlastingly expatiating on the heavenly loveliness of service, but who never takes the trouble to tell his people in unambiguous English what they ought to do.

It must be confessed that not a few ministers fail because of their inherent and ineradicable selfishness. They work for the building of their own throne, and give little thought to the thrones of their brethren. Their ambition, perhaps, is to make their pulpit a throne, and they count themselves the only preacher, forgetting that there ought to be in every parish as many heralds of the cross as there are

Christians, and that it is only when the entire church is at work preaching that the whole parish can be reached. It may be their ambition to be model pastors, and they devote themselves to the building of lofty pastoral thrones, forgetting that there ought to be in their churches as many pastors as there are members. To every Christian is given the responsibility of shepherding souls. The pastor is a shepherd of shepherds. Because the minister alone officiates at the Lord's Table, he may lose sight of the fact that every Christian is a priest, and is anointed to be a mediator between God and men. It is easy for a minister to be selfish without realizing how selfish he is. He may insist on doing everything himself, because he is unwilling to submit to the drudgery of training others. He may prefer to do all the speaking at every meeting because he has not the patience to develop in others the gift of speech. A man of this type gradually gathers up everything into his own hands, his people degenerating into auditors and spectators. But his sin finds him out. By failing to develop the resources of his people, he curtails the sphere of his influence. The man who builds masterful workers multiplies himself manyfold. A preacher is never so surely adding cubits to the height of his own throne as when he is building thrones for his brethren. It is by surrounding his throne by other thrones that he comes into the fulness of the power which has been promised.

How, then, shall the minister go to work in the construction of thrones? He must first of all believe in human nature. He must have faith in the capacity of the average man. God alone knows the soul and the extent of its undiscovered resources. The preacher who builds his hopes on brilliant people only is doomed to disappointment. The five-talented men and women are few in number, and even when they use their talents, they are inadequate to the situation. The preacher who would make his church a power must begin by trusting common people. The man with two talents must be cultivated, and the man with one talent must not be neglected. Stupid people are bright people not yet awakened. Mediocre folk are geniuses whose hour has not yet come. You never know how many talents a man has from what he says or from what he is able to exhibit. One of the constant surprises in this world is the way in which the people from whom we had expected little surpass those from whom we had expected much. The pigmies are always springing into giants, the dull pupils are constantly passing the best examinations, the

sluggards are continually shaking off their lethargy
and performing the labors of Hercules.   It is the old
story, the tortoise arrives before the hare.   The
race is not always to the man you call swift, and the
battle is not always to the man you think strong.
God seems to take delight in surprising us by choosing "the foolish things of the world to shame them
that are wise, and the weak things of the world to
put to shame the things that are strong, and the
base things of the world, and the things that are
despised, yea and the things that are not to bring
to nought the things that are."   To unlock the vital
energies of immortal souls and set them working in
our human world is a work fit for a god.   Many a
preacher fails because he underestimates the possibilities of his people.   All of them are created in
God's image.   All of them are heirs of immortality.
All of them are bought by the blood of Jesus.   They
are now sons of God and it does not yet appear what
they shall be even this side of death.   We only
know that they can pass from glory to glory,
gaining more and more of the power of the Lord.
Some ministers can use old people, but not young
people.   They are suspicious of their young people,
and quarrel with them.   Others can coöperate with
men, but not with women.   They disparage feminine

endowments and lack ability to make use of them. Others can utilize the educated, but not the unlettered, the rich but not the poor, or *vice versa;* but the successful preacher draws boldly on the resources of all. He puts to use the vigor and hopefulness of the young, the retrospection and wisdom of the old, the virility of men and the tenderness of women, the vivacity of youth and the innocence of children, for out of the mouths of babes and sucklings God still perfects praise. He renders useful the rich and the cultured, and also the servants and all who hew wood and draw water, remembering that the spirit of God has come upon all flesh, and that every human being is a shekinah.

Show your faith in human nature by expecting the largest things of your people. Give them abundant and taxing work to do. A church that is not kept busy is certain to become fastidious, and a church given to criticising is a church that encumbers the ground. There is nothing so deadly to the spirit of faultfinding, and the entire brood of demons to which faultfinding gives birth, as work. Work develops what is best in us, and kills what is worst. You can cast out demons by training men to labor. Work is a great socializer. It breaks down barriers. Important work must be done by coöperative effort. Coöperation increases strength and also good feeling. Girls who sew together for the poor sew their hearts together. Women who plan and pray for missionaries forget their social differences. Large tasks call for the strength of the group, and with the coming of Christians into groups there descends the spirit of power. Association in labor is a means of grace. Morbid moods disappear and bad heart habits are sloughed off in an atmosphere made warm by social intercourse. Church work accomplishes many things, and not the least is the bringing of Christians together. By coming together they get nearer to God.

Trust the people, give them work, and then be patient with them. The important thing is not that things be done superbly, but that they be done increasingly well. The head of a church must not be fussy and must have the love which suffers long and still is kind. Many of those who enter the vineyard will slink out of it before noon, discouraged. Others will stand idle in the vineyard, preferring the shade of the vineyard to the sun of the market-place. Your first impulse will be to castigate. But castigation is not a preacher's occupation. He is an encourager. People need nothing so much as courage. A scolding pastor lessens the courage even of the brave. The faint-hearted are legion, and to scorn them is a sin. The blunderers must not be whipped. Mistakes are numerous and exasperating, but after all a minister with eyes can always see a lot of solid strength and splendid promise. To recognize a success is better than to call attention to a failure. To blow a trumpet over a victory is better tactics than to play a flute over a defeat. Fix your eyes on the best things. It is an encouragement to preachers that Christ had such a fondness for a grain of mustard seed. What wonderful eyes he had for seeing the possibilities wrapped up in diminutive bundles. A preacher needs the eyes of Jesus, for oftentimes the encouraging symptoms in the parish are no larger than mustard seeds. He also needs the heart of Jesus. A bruised reed our Lord would not break. A smoking wick he would not extinguish. There come days when to the preacher's eyes there are no reeds in sight except bruised reeds, and no wicks except those that are smoking. The church seems filled with smoke, and the preacher is at the point of choking. But a builder, working under a permit granted by Heaven upon a structure which is to outlast the stars, ought not to become discouraged. He ought to count the cost before he begins. Erecting thrones requires the qualities which a builder needs in the building of a palace or a tower. It takes time and skill, fidelity and patience. It cannot be done in a month or a year. It cannot be accomplished without thought. It requires a sweat of blood. It is impossible without something of the calm-eyed perseverance and the persistent courage and the sober joy which Jesus had in the building of the thrones for his apostles. The working force of the church can be indefinitely increased by a minister who has mastered the secrets of the art of building. Energies can be coördinated, influences can be mobilized, power can be built, if only the laws of God are known and followed.

Keep your church, then, at the centre of the world. Let the concentric circle, marking off the different zones, lie always luminous in your eyes: Jerusalem, your town, Judea, your country, Samaria, those provinces of your nation's life least permeated with spiritual forces, and finally the great non-christian world. This is your parish. The man who goes into his pulpit with these spheres of influence spread out before him will not be likely to let his people go to sleep. There will come into his utterance the tone that Demosthenes knew, and men will say to one another, while he preaches, "Let us march against Philip!" It is for the preacher to pick up his congregation and hurl it upon the world. The work of the preacher is with his church, the work of the church is with the world. Let the preacher concentrate himself upon his church, and his church will take hold of the town, the nation, and the nations. Ministers who rush hither and thither, eaten up with reformatory zeal, meddling with this and dabbling with that, do not begin to do so much for the advancement of the Kingdom of God as do the men who stay at home and pour out into the souls of their own people the full measure of their vitality and devotion. What spectacle is more lamentable than that of a minister struggling by vociferous speech on miscellaneous platforms to reform society, when his own church is scrawny and feeble; striving to set the world on fire when the little group of people whom God has intrusted to his keeping are chalky and limp. The church is the preacher's throne, and the man who builds the most vigorous and puissant church wields the longest sceptre and wears the brightest crown.

There are seven forms of power which a Christian church should be possessor of, or rather there are seven kingdoms in which its influence should be felt.

The church is first of all a worshipping body. She sings praises and offers prayers unto God. She cultivates the devotional life and trains men to bow

N

their heads and hearts before the King of heaven. Public worship is a force to be carefully safeguarded and constantly strengthened. A church becomes a more effective working church when it has once learned to pray and sing. Bringing the heart to the throne of grace increases all its capacities and makes it capable of larger service. Public worship, moreover, is the testimony which the church bears to the community of its faith in the God who has revealed himself in Christ. For this reason, public worship should be full-toned and jubilant. Paul was always concerned about the impression which the church in her worship might make upon a visiting stranger. All preachers who have the Pauline wisdom plan and labor for the improvement of their church worship. To give it a richer and more penetrating tone, to impart to it a higher beauty, to suffuse it with a more solemnizing and subduing spirit, is to increase the power of the church, not only over the lives of its members, but over the feeling of the community. Church attendance is not for Christians an elective. It is an essential part of the confession which a follower of Jesus makes to the world, a part of the work which the Master expects him to perform. The very existence of Christianity depends on social worship, as all the persecuting Roman emperors well understood. Could Christians not come together, the power of the Prince of Glory would be broken. "Forsake not the assembling of yourselves together," — so wrote a New Testament writer to men who ran the risk of losing their lives by frequenting the assemblies of the Nazarene. Worship does a mighty work. It melts the hearts of men together. They forget their differences of rank and culture and fortune when they repeat the creed or bow their heads in prayer. For the effacing of the lines which separate and the obliteration of the barriers which estrange, there is an immeasurable potency in common prayer. A congregation devoutly engaged in worship is doing something for the community which cannot be done in any other way. It is a collective confession of Christ which outruns in influence the confession of any one individual, no matter how exalted. It has a power which the mightiest of sermons cannot exert. A careless or dwindled congregation retards the progress of Christianity. A lifeless and formal worship shuts the heavens and makes it difficult to believe what Christ has said. Desultory church attendance is in Christians a sin. No Christian can absent himself needlessly from public worship without damaging the influence of the Christian society and

bringing loss to his own soul. Such persons are to
be accounted disorderly. They have left their place
in the ranks. They have violated the law of love.
They are to be admonished. The preacher cannot
afford to allow the worship in his church to become
ragged or meagre. High standards should be held
up. The Lord's army on the Lord's day should
present a solid front. A disorderly or decimated
army suggests demoralization and invites defeat.
Public worship is a form of power. It is one of the
lights in the seven-branched candlestick.

The Christian society is a teaching body. The
preacher is a teacher. The church is a school. The
name for his followers which the Master loved was
pupils. History knows him as the Great Teacher.
The minister is the head teacher of his church, but
he cannot do his work without assistants. What
head teacher can? He must educate a body of men
and women to whom God has given the teaching
gift and place them upon thrones. At stated times
the church meets for the study of the Scriptures
by question and answer. Such a session of the
church we call the Bible school. Whatever its name,
it should not be forgotten that the school is not an
outside institution, or an appendage to the church,
but that it is the church itself engaged in the study

of the Bible. The children are pupils and so also
are the parents. The young are there and so also
are heads which are hoary. The school includes
professing Christians and all others who are willing
to be taught. Here is an opportunity for the
preacher to enlarge the scope of the church's influence. By calling into the work of Bible teaching
a company of Christians variously gifted, a wider
and deeper impression is made than could be produced by any one man. The choosing and training
of these teachers is a task of stupendous importance.
Through the personalities of the teachers, the gospel
comes with a wide variety of richness and persuasive-
ness, supplementing the instruction of the pulpit
and reaching recesses in the community into which
sermons could not travel. Boys and girls who might
never be influenced by pulpit discourses, or even by
the prayers of their parents, are often wooed and
won by the fidelity and love of a teacher; and fathers
and mothers who had lost all interest in organized
Christianity frequently take their places in the pew
again, because their children are in the Bible school.
The preacher who raises up a consecrated Bible
teacher opens a new channel for the inflow of God's
grace. No Christians grow so rapidly as those who
teach the Bible. It is the Bible teachers who become

the pillars of the church. In training teachers for
their work the preacher is building thrones. Bible
teaching is a second flame in the golden candlestick.

The church is an evangelizing body. It exists
to make converts. The Master called men to him
only to send them out. He sent forth every one who
took his yoke and learned of him. St. Luke tells
us that all the members of the church in Jerusalem
went forth preaching the word. Every Christian
is a witness. The purpose of his witnessing is to
bring others to the truth. A church which makes
no converts is a church which Christ cannot own.
Unless it adds to the number of those who are being
saved, its own life is forfeited. It is sometimes
asked if a pastor ought to be an evangelist? If by
evangelist is meant a man whose business it is to tell
the good news in such a way as to bring men to
Christ, then certainly every minister is called to do
the work of an evangelist. His pulpit message
should never lose the evangelistic note. His words
should pierce men's hearts and bring them to repentance. His appeals ought to prick men's consciences and compel them to ask what they ought to
do. If a minister preaches an entire year to uncon-
verted people without a conversion, it is time that
he withdraw from the ministry or ask God to give

him another heart. But the preacher is not the only evangelist. Laymen are baptized to announce the good tidings. It is their privilege and their duty to lead men into the kingdom of God. Church members must be trained to do evangelistic work. They are not likely to do it unless they are asked. They cannot do it well unless they are trained. It is for the preacher to gather round him a body of evangelists and send them forth heralding the King. Laymen can reach hearts which are closed to the preacher. They can speak with an accent which the preacher does not possess. The minister who trains a body of lay preachers extends immeasurably the range of the church's power. No one man has sufficient compass to his voice to reach all classes of people. There should be a varied appeal coming through the tongues of many consecrated believers. The church is an evangelist, and the evangel ought to break into music on a multitude of tongues. Passion for souls is a power. Evangelism is another candle in our beautiful candlestick.

The church is a humanitarian body, — a servant of the human race. Jesus was a lover of human beings, irrespective of their condition or relations, and his church is bound to show good-will toward all. There are three classes which must be ever close to the

church's heart, because they are dear to the heart of
Jesus, — the sick, the poor, and the forsaken. Nothing so enraged his soul as inhumanity. He began his
public ministry by declaring his mission to be preaching the gospel to the poor, healing the broken-hearted,
preaching deliverance to the captives, and recovering
of sight to the blind, and setting at liberty them that
are bruised. When John the Baptist sent inquiring
whether he was indeed the Messiah, the reply of
Jesus was, "Tell him I am doing deeds of mercy."
He declared that the universe was built on this
principle, and that the only men who would be
counted blessed on the Judgment Day would be
those who had ministered to the sick and the poor
and the forsaken. A preacher is not fit to preach
who has no time to visit the sick, to help the poor,
and to befriend the forlorn and neglected. If a
preacher has not the spirit of Christ, he is none of
his, no matter what he says in the pulpit. But this
work cannot be done by the preacher alone. All
Christians must share in the privilege, that they may
become partakers of the heavenly rewards. The
philanthropic work of the church should be organized, and the largest possible number of church members should be enlisted in it. Most of them will
not go into it of their own accord. They must be

called to it by the pastor and trained by him that they may do it well. It is for him to perform the miracle of multiplying the pairs of consecrated hands until the entire community feels the church's healing touch. The church is a philanthropist. Social service is a power. Philanthropy is an additional flame-jet in the genial and hospitable candlestick.

The church is a reforming body. Its mission is to turn the world upside down. It must prepare the way of the Lord and make his paths straight. It must torment the demons before their time. It must put its foot upon serpents and scorpions. It must be known as the implacable foe of things evil. The strongholds of iniquity must be attacked, and if possible pulled down. The ideal minister is a warrior. He brings not peace but a sword. He will make bad men fear him, he will lay siege to the particular evils of his own town. Those of antiquity may be referred to in a parenthesis, and so may those of a city a hundred miles away. The preacher must decide as to which enemies shall be first assaulted, and then proceed to lay plans for accomplishing their overthrow. But the preacher cannot fight alone. He is only a general, and no general fights without his army. The church is an army. This was Paul's conception. To Timothy he wrote,

"War a good warfare." This assumes that a
preacher is a leader in a long campaign. Some
preachers have a deal to say about the church militant, but their churches do no fighting. A church
which does not fight is a church whose pastor is not a
general. An army never fights unless it is organized
on a fighting basis, and is commanded by a man
who is not averse to battle. The church is the force
with which the preacher is to wage war. He must
drill his soldiers in the art of fighting. Many a community is cursed with abuses which might be thrown
off, if only the churches would stir themselves. The
churches would put on the armor, if only they had
generals with a genius for command. Hundreds
of young men might have been saved to the church,
had only the preachers of the town picked out some
one formidable fortress of the enemy, and organized
the fighting ability of the youth for a vigorous and
thrilling campaign. Young men want something to
do. By the grace of God they are born fighters. If
the church were only more militant, it might event-
ually even in this world become triumphant. Spiritual militarism is a form of power. Zeal for reform
is a fifth lamp in the glorious candlestick.

Can the church be a political force? If by political
force is meant a force influencing the temper and con-

duct of government, the answer is, Yes. Politics is one of the kingdoms of life, and the church is to be a power in all of the kingdoms. A preacher is a teacher of duty, and no class of duties can be counted trivial or unclean. For a preacher to slur or over-look political obligations is to be recreant to his trust. Men are to render to Cæsar the things which are Cæsar's. The officers of the state are ministers of God, and the work which they perform is a part of the plan of the Eternal. Church and state are in a sense separate, but spiritually they are united by indissoluble bonds. They act and react upon each other, and both are divine agencies ordained for the education of mankind. Each must help the other to be what it ought to be. The church must be held steadily at the center of the political world. The mind of Christ must be built into the state.

This does not mean that the preacher shall cham-pion favorite candidates, or defend party platforms, or advocate partisan programmes. Party meetings are always out of place in a Christian church, and party sermons are always mischievous in a Christian pulpit. The minister who attempts to dictate to men how they shall vote, or who ventures even to advise a course of political action, is certain to suffer the retribution which his temerity has invited. Why should a preacher be so short-sighted as to entangle himself with policies and parties, when he can do a work so much greater by rousing souls to a sense of civic obligation? Why try to build a political party, when one can build a political power? Why not be content to quicken civic conscience, exalt civic duties, keep social problems ever before men's eyes, infuse the spirit of Christ into political discussion, so frame the sermons that forces shall leap out of them generating devotion to civic ends? The minister is a prophet of the Lord. His work is inspirational. He is a builder of sentiments, a creator of atmospheres. It is for him to strengthen sentiments which will strangle politicians of the baser sort, and create an atmosphere in which many a boss and heeler will meet political death by asphyxiation. His work is to enlarge the social mind, the mind that concerns itself with communal affairs, and that labors to extend the laws of Christ over widening areas of life. Let him kindle a passion for social justice, intensify the hunger for civic righteousness, and make men daring in the face of depressing situations. Man is a political animal. His political nature must be stimulated and set free. A religion which leaves the political interests and activities of men outside its jurisdiction is not a religion which will commend itself to twentieth century men. The church must penetrate everything — even the world of the politicians. Passion for civic righteousness is another torch in the blazing candlestick.

The church is a missionary body, it is sent on an errand to the whole creation. To a Christian a narrow life is forbidden. The church is a body of missionaries, organized for the purpose of sending their thoughts and prayers and assistance to human beings whom they have never seen. It is by the constant forwarding of messages of good-will and tokens of love that isolated congregations are bound together and chasms between races are bridged. The missionary force of a church can be amazingly multiplied and extended. Everything depends on the minister. If the thoughts of his people do not reach round the world, and if their hearts are not sufficiently capacious to hold all nations and races, it is because his own vision is narrow and he is lacking in the skill to call out of the heart the forces which are deepest and mightiest. The preacher who informs himself in regard to missionary heroes and labors, who keeps before his people missionary principles, motives, problems, and victories, who organizes classes among the old and the young for the study of current movements in the missionary world, will in time create a body of missionary sentiment which will make itself felt to the ends of the earth. The smallest and poorest congregation can be trained to carry on its heart, if not a continent, at least an island in a distant sea. Missionary enthusiasm is another luminous wick in the God-created candlestick.

These are seven ways in which the church brings its life to bear upon the world. They are seven beams of light streaming out across human lives and homes, calling men to glorify their Father who is in heaven. They are seven thrones on each one of which Christ is seated, asserting his sovereignty over the affairs of men. The lights, if you look at them long enough, all blend into one light, and the thrones, if you consider them intently, mass themselves into one throne. The one light is the light that shines from God in the face of Jesus Christ, and the one throne is the seat of the King who wears many crowns. The preacher who, by giving his life to his church, makes it potent in all the kingdoms of human thought and activity, has sat down with the King of kings in his throne.

LECTURE VI

THE HOLY CATHOLIC CHURCH

THE HOLY CATHOLIC CHURCH

THUS far we have been dealing with the local congregation. Let us now consider the relation of the congregation to other congregations of the same communion, and the relation of these communions to other communions of the universal church. No congregation lives to itself or dies to itself. It is part of an organism, intimately knit up with other bodies, forming a living whole. A pastor is bound to take heed to all the flock in which the Holy Ghost has made him a bishop or overseer, and he must so conduct his work as to feed the great church of God of which his particular flock is a tiny fragment. Every preacher should do his work in the radiance of the vision of the church universal. Thus labored the first great preacher, Paul. He beheld the church always looming before him as an august and heavenly creation, at present stained and marred by human imperfection, but growing up into One able to make it a glorious church, not having spot or wrinkle or any such thing. Belief in the Holy Catholic church is one of the articles of the universal creed, and the preacher who links his belief in the church with his belief in God the Father, Son, and Holy Spirit, works with an unfailing energy and keeps his heart serene in the midst of the storms.

There is but one church known to the New Testament. Christ never conceived of more than one. His church is a temple and it is built upon one foundation. It is a vine of which he is the stock, and believers are branches. Two vines are unthought of. It is a flock, and while there may be many folds, there can never be more than one flock under the care of one Shepherd. Dissensions and divisions were the one evil against which Jesus threw his heart in his high-priestly prayer, on the last night. That his church may be one is the deep and constant longing of his soul.

All of St. Paul's metaphors are stamped with the idea of unity. He sees but one temple, one pillar, one body, one bride, one household, one medium of revelation. When enemies filled the world with rumors that he and the apostles in Palestine were building on different foundations, he hastened to Jerusalem, and by a public conference with his brother workers endeavored to put an end to the damaging insinuations. He knew that a divided church could never win the world. He who builds on a separate foundation toils in vain.

But by unity is not meant uniformity, either of government or of polity or of ritual. Uniformity is a surface thing, unity is deep and vital. "That they may be one in us," which being interpreted means one in character, fellowship, spirit, love, so runs Jesus' great prayer, and it is the same sort of unity which Paul has in mind when he exhorts the Ephesians to give diligence "to keep the unity of the Spirit in the bond of peace." To Paul, as to all other New Testament writers, "There is one body, and one Spirit, one Lord, one faith, one baptism, one God and Father of all." The unity is not formal, but spiritual.

This spiritual unity manifests itself outwardly, but not perfectly. The treasure is in an earthen vessel, and the vessel bears the flaws of its origin. But the unity is none the less real. Imperfection mars, but does not destroy, genuine spiritual possessions, either in individuals or organizations. The unity of the church is a growing unity, and passes gradually from less to more. "Each separate building, fitly framed together, is growing into a holy temple in the Lord." The unity will express itself in completer manifestations in the successive stages of the unfolding process, until all groups of Christians "attain unto the unity of the faith and of the knowledge of the Son of God, unto a full-grown man, unto the measure of the stature of the fulness of Christ." If all Christians are only rooted and grounded in love, then all will grow up sometime, somehow, in all things into him which is the Head, even Christ.

The real unity of the Christian church in the twentieth century is a fact which every preacher ought to see, and proclaim with joy. Many sour-eyed prophets have gone abroad, bewailing in lugubrious tones the church's deplorable and diabolical divisions, and by their exaggerated representations have caused many even of the elect to forget sundry things which ought to be held steadily in mind. The church of Christ is not so divided as it looks. The confusion is neither so deep nor deadly as it has been painted. The seamless robe of Christ is not so badly torn as the disconsolate are asserting. In ritual and discipline and government the various bodies of the Lord's people differ, as they have a right to do, but in the things which are essential they are deeply and gloriously united. It is not by differences in conception of God and Christ and the Holy Spirit, of character and duty and destiny, but chiefly by divergent views in regard to forms of ecclesiastical administration that the various Christian communions are held apart. There is a surprising unity in all

the branches of Christendom in the things which are
fundamental. All Christians of whatever name unite
in repeating the Prayer which the Lord taught, and
in their extempore petitions they pray substantially,
not only for the same things, but largely in similar
or identical phrases. Every Christian pulpit has
in it the same text-book, the Bible. The words of
prophets and apostles and the Lord himself are in
every church the same. All Christian bodies sing
hymns made sweet by the name of Jesus. In nearly
all the hymn-books church union has already been
consummated. Christian ministers of every ecclesiastical fellowship baptize men into the name of the
Father, the Son, and the Holy Spirit, and make use of
the bread and the wine in obedience to Him who
died for all. All the great branches of the Christian
church repeat the Apostles' Creed. All Christian
communions produce with minor variations the same
general type of character. The Christian saints, no
matter whence they come, are brothers, and carry in
their faces the same superscription. All Christians
set before them the same model — Jesus of Nazareth.
There is an expanding fellowship in work. The
Protestant denominations are at the end of each dec-
ade closer together in Christian service, and all the
Christian bodies the world over, when not degenerate,

perform similar works of mercy.   In every commun-
ion of the great church, Jesus Christ is the acknowl-
edged Head.   His name is above every name.   All
Christendom prostrates itself before One alone, Jesus
Christ, proclaimed in sermon, prayer, and song the
King of Kings and Lord of Lords.

The glory of the church universal ought to shine
round a man in the hour in which he is deciding which
one of the various households of the common faith
he shall make his home.   It is a matter of critical
moment, both for the man himself and the cause of
Christ, that the young minister shall throw his life
into that particular Christian group which shall enable him to render largest service to the church
universal.   He should keep out of denominations
which have no solid reason for their continued separate existence, and give his strength to a communion which is testifying with conspicuous effectiveness to a truth which the great church needs, and
which is keeping alive in the world a principle which
mankind cannot afford to let die.   Protestantism
is needlessly divided, and the time has arrived when
many of the smaller denominations, having accomplished the specific purpose for which they were born,
should surrender their corporate existence in the interest of a more effective Christianity.   Young men

of education and power cannot afford to identify themselves with organizations which only needlessly complicate the doing of the church's business, and which render a feeble and dwindling testimony to the great doctrines of the Christian faith. A man is under obligation to link his life in with men who are doing something indispensable and enduringly valuable for the Kingdom of God.

Having decided upon his denomination, the preacher must then consider to what particular parish he shall give himself. Here again a wise decision cannot be rendered without taking into account the Holy Catholic Church. The minister is under obligation to go to that one of the congregations which call him in which he can render largest service to the great church. It may be in the city or in the village, in some older section of the country or on its frontier, in the homeland or beyond the sea; it may be a large church or a small church, a rich church or a poor church, but the one thing essential is that it shall give unimpeded scope for the free exercise of the gifts of a full-grown man. The young preacher cannot allow himself to go into a community which is overchurched, and to become the pastor of an organization which is not needed. He should not listen to any advisers who counsel him to squeeze himself into a narrow place, for the sake of maintaining the prestige of his denomination, or of carrying out the ambitious plan of some shortsighted, overzealous missionary secretary. The needless multiplication of churches is a wicked folly, and in many a community all the churches but one ought to be allowed to die. To kill them outright by ecclesiastical vote, is at present an impossibility, but young ministers can possibly hasten their death by keeping away from them. In a world so needy as this, with multitudinous, urgent tasks calling for men, it is a tragic blunder for a young man to accept the pastorate of a church in which it is not possible for him to make his life count in the work of his generation. Such a course is ruinous in every way. The preacher himself becomes dwarfed in spirit and stunted in intellect. He and his wife are likely to wear out their hearts in trying to live upon a salary totally inadequate to their needs. Moreover, the dispositions created in small communities in which competing churches struggle for precedence, watching one another's every movement with eyes like those of jealous animals, are states of mind which are totally contrary to those which the Gospel is intended to foster, and render the coming of the kingdom of righteousness and peace and joy an utter impossi-

bility.   Keep away from the church that has no excuse for its existence save inherited bigotry or denominational pride.   A village church, or a country
church, if it commands the field, is a great opportunity for any man, no matter how wondrously gifted.
Because a church is poor or small is no reason why
a seminary graduate should turn his back upon it,
provided it has a field.   But to throw one's self away
in the attempt to keep the breath of life in one
of six churches in a community which needs but one
or two, is a piece of foolishness for which there is no
justification.   It is not self-sacrifice, it is suicide.

Having chosen your denomination and your
parish, throw yourself into your church in such a
way as to make it a power among the churches with
which it is connected in a common service.   A
preacher should never be ashamed of his denomination, nor should he underestimate it.   Denominationalism is just now receiving many stripes, for its
limitations and bitter fruits are numerous and conspicuous.   But after the worst has been said, it
remains a fact that denominationalism has brought
upon the church of Christ innumerable and immeasurable blessings.   The revolt from Rome in the
sixteenth century was not a mistake.   The course
pursued by Calvin was not a blunder.   The re-

fusal of the Puritans to submit to the tyranny and
insolence of the Anglican Bishops was not an act
to be apologized for by their descendants. The
freeing of the Wesleyan movement from the Anglican
church was ordained of God. It is written large
across the face of the modern world that where the
church is most diversely organized, there is it most
alive. Uniformity like a bewitching dream still
haunts many minds, but it is an *ignis fatuus* which
leads nations into quagmires. It is where the church
is most uniform that spiritual vitality is least abundant. The religious outlook is more favorable in
Germany than in Russia, brighter in England than
in Germany, more promising in the United States
than in England. God seems to love variety in the
church, as he loves it in the fields and in the sky.
Liberty in the choice of ritual and government
may create a temporary and disconcerting confusion,
but it ministers mightily to life and progress. If
by its fruits, then, we are to judge denominationalism
the conclusion is unescapable that it has met inexorable needs of a growing world. No man need be
ashamed of belonging to a sect. The Roman Catholic and Episcopal churches, no less than the Methodist and Baptist churches, are sects, sections of the
great Church of God. The Greek church, the Church

of Rome, the Lutheran church, and the Church of England, no less than the Presbyterian and Congregational churches, are denominations, groups of believers in the great Household of Faith. There is no more reason why a man should be ashamed of belonging to a sect, than of belonging to a regiment in an army. It is only by division and subdivision that an army is rendered effective, and so it is only by grouping Christians around regimental standards that the church of Christ at the present stage of development becomes manageable and capable of doing its largest work. A soldier does not show disrespect to the army when he is loyal to his regiment. By regimental loyalty he increases the efficiency of the army. His value to the army is measured by his fidelity to his own division commander. It is only when the separate regiments are kept to a high standard of action, that the army comes into possession of conquering power. Every preacher is most loyal to the whole church of Christ when he is most faithful to his own denomination. The two are not contradictory, but denominational fidelity is an essential condition of catholic effectiveness. A preacher who is so puffed up by vague ideas of liberality as to be indifferent to the welfare and progress of his own denomination, is a preacher who needlessly circumscribes his influence and incapacitates himself for rendering the largest service to the universal church.   It is by the careful training of his church in the art of keeping step with the other churches of his regiment, that he makes his most valuable contribution to the fighting strength of the army of the Lord of Hosts.

Ministers in the early years of their ministry ought to be diligent students of their denominational literature.   They ought to know how their denomination came to be, the truths which it has emphasized, the principles which it has glorified, the work which it has accomplished, and the heroes and saints whom it has presented to the world.   They ought to familiarize themselves with the genius and features of its organization, and the methods of its ecclesiastical procedure, paying particular attention to the achievements and present enterprises of all its missionary organizations.   No society can live and work without machinery.   Machinery is run by men.   To help run the denominational machinery is a part of the preacher's work.   If he shirks it, he shows himself to be a selfish man.   Laymen are not to be excused from work which they do not like, neither are preachers.   If ministers preach self-sacrifice, they ought to practise it.   Denominational meetings may not be always interesting, and the details of administrative business may be irksome, but loyalty to his denomination is one of the most beautiful of all the ministerial virtues, and to sacrifice his time and strength for the good of the related churches is evidence that the preacher is a Christian man. If ministers accept the emoluments and honors which come to them as members of a noble branch of the church of God, and leave the routine and necessary ecclesiastical work to their more unselfish brothers, it is because their conscience is undeveloped, and they have never been instructed in one of the most important of all the departments of clerical obligation and service.

Denominational loyalty brings certain disciplines which render men more effective in the pulpit. It is a good thing for a preacher to know his ministerial brethren, especially those who are not his equals in attainments or position. The humblest and most commonplace servant of the Lord honestly toiling in the obscurest field, is not unworthy the companionship of the most exalted of the pulpit princes. God still loves the humble and the unnoticed, and the man who would preach with searching power must keep near to those whom God loves. A preacher needs the widened heart, for preaching is

primarily a business of the heart. It is a means of
grace for a minister to know and love his brethren,
high and low, his comrades in the arduous warfare,
his coworkers in a hard field. He can afford to give
time and thought — no matter how large his parish
— to those who are pledged with him to support the
great cause. It is good also to face strong men in
meetings in which delicate business is transacted
and estranging questions are debated. A preacher
needs to encounter the views of able men who differ
from him, and to listen to speeches advocating
positions to which he is vigorously opposed. Denominational conferences, assemblies, and councils,
are a school in which the pulpit servants of the Lord
receive a training which can be gotten nowhere else.
A preacher is always speaking to people who are held
by church etiquette from publicly expressing dissent,
and, therefore, he above all men needs to face from
time to time an audience which will not hesitate to
tear his arguments to tatters, and vote down his
most cherished propositions. Instead of retreating
into his parish and submerging himself in parochial
affairs, he needs to go out into the denominational
world, and grapple with those larger problems in
which thousands of churches are interested, and to
combat, if necessary, in the open arena, ideas and

tendencies which in his judgment do not make for the advancement of the Kingdom. It is dwarfing for a man to get so interested in his own congregation that he loses sight of the multitude of congregations whose life is bound up with that of his own. He ought to lift up his eyes and look, and train his people to lift up their eyes and look, upon the great company of comrades with whom they are marching. It is for him to develop in his people a denominational consciousness, a quickened sense that they belong to others. The bonds must be strengthened between his church and its sister churches. His church must be kept in touch with the movement of the entire body to which it belongs. Denominational opportunities and problems and enterprises ought to be given a conspicuous place, and the sweep of the preacher's thought should keep his hearers alive to the fact that they are a part of an interested company engaged in a common work, and moving toward a common goal.

When a congregation falls out of sympathy with its sister congregations, and wraps itself up completely in its own local tasks, it is the fault of the preacher. An isolated preacher insulates his church. The currents of the common life do not flow through him or his people. Such a preacher is not a builder. He can mould and place a piece of stucco, but he cannot construct a segment of a great arch. The vaulting spiritual relationships and the overarching sympathies and unities which hung always before the eye of the master-builder of Tarsus are clean beyond his ken. Alas for the preacher whose uttermost horizon is the narrow boundary of his own little parish. Why should not every preacher so live and labor as to help shape the ideals and dispositions of his entire regiment? To influence one's denomination, however, one must pay the price. The price is self-sacrificing loyalty, honest and self-abnegating service. A preacher cannot influence his brethren unless he loves them. He cannot stand high in the denominational councils unless he serves. If any man is to be great among the churches of his order, he must become the servant of all.

Here again a plea is made for narrowness in the interest of breadth. The preacher is to concentrate his powers upon his congregation for the sake of his denomination. He is to exalt and adorn his denomination for the sake of the Holy Catholic Church. If his denomination suffers, then all the denominations suffer with it; or if his denomination is honored, then all have reason to rejoice with it. The various denominations constitute the body of Christ, and are members in particular. There should, therefore, be no schism, but the denominations should have the same care one for another. Each denomination does something which no other can do quite so well. Each performs a function which ministers to the life of all. Differing widely in form and structure, they yet belong to one another. There are diversities of workings, but it is the same God who worketh all things in all. The eye ought not to say to the hand, "I have no need of thee," nor again the head to the feet, "I have no need of you." Even denominations which seem to be feeble may for the present be necessary, and deserve a more abundant honor. There are diversities of gifts, but the same Spirit. And there are diversities of ministrations, and the same Lord. To each one is given the manifestation of the Spirit to profit withal. Having gifts differing according to the grace that was given, every denomination ought to do superbly the particular thing which it feels called to do, not for its own self-aggrandizement, but for the enrichment of the universal church. If a denomination feels itself intrusted with the work of emphasizing a particular truth, then the better its work is performed, the sooner will other denominations be impressed by that truth, and be induced to give it place in their own

P

teaching and practice. If a principle is indeed a thought of God, and one branch of the church is led by the Spirit to give it a wider application in human life, then with every increase in the strength of this branch of the church comes a fresh power of this principle in its operation in the life of the whole. Every denomination intrusted with a special grace owes it to all the other denominations so to incarnate the heavenly treasure as to make it seem a desirable possession. Love does not require that men shall suppress their deepest convictions, and keep silence in regard to truths which the Holy Spirit has to them made clear. It is only by the brave and persistent affirmation of those things which keep welling up in the heart, that the whole truth finds expression and the church of God becomes the medium for the transmission of an unmutilated message. It is for the great church that each branch of the church lives and labors. Sectarianism of the baser sort begins with the sect and ends there. It is the conceit of the branch affirming that it is the vine. Denominationalism is always a curse when it lifts the denomination above the church universal. It is not more disgraceful to belong to a sect than it is for a leaf to grow on a twig or for a twig to grow on a branch, but it is disgraceful for the leaf to forget the twig, and for the branch to imagine it is the tree. Sectarianism when baptized into the spirit of Jesus ends with the great church. The branch drinks in the sun and the rain in order to add vigor and fruitfulness to the tree. It is fidelity to the great whole which saves the parts from pettiness and decay.

The preacher needs this vision to keep the gospel vital on his lips. Only men of capacious heart can preach with power the message which thrilled prophets and apostles. It is a scandal in the Christian church when a minister is a petty man. A thin and stunted personality cannot be a fit channel for the heavenly grace. Conceited pedants, opinionated snobs, and supercilious dandies may stand in a Christian pulpit, but they cannot preach the Gospel. The Gospel is the message of the broadminded, sweet-hearted, lofty-spirited, brotherly Son of God. To make himself large enough to transmit even a little of the Master's spirit is a true preacher's lifelong ambition and unending struggle. The great sentences of the New Testament shrivel on the lips of narrow-headed zealots, who excommunicate their brethren who differ from them. In the eyes of God, he is both heretic and schismatic who by word or action breaks the law of love. The preacher who wishes to preach with the apostolic accent must breathe the atmosphere in which the apostles did their work. He must come under the power of Him who is the express image of the infinitely sympathetic and all-embracing God. Devotion to the church ought to add cubits to a man's spiritual stature and new diameters to the circle of his sympathies. If the word ecclesiastic has taken on a dark and sinister meaning, it is only an added proof of the wizardry of the mystery of evil which is able to corrupt human hearts even when engaged with things holiest and highest.

It is wholesome to form the habit of speaking of the church as the Church of God. The phrase is apostolic and breathes a majesty and elevation which adjectives coined in denominational mints are likely to obscure. Along with the books which deal with the history and teachings of his own denomination, the preacher should find room for volumes telling the story of other communions which have also borne the burden, and which are making certain by their sacrifices the ultimate triumph of Christ. In no branch of the Christian church has God left himself without a witness, and if we are to judge religious organizations by their fruits, then all of them have won his favor, for all have received manifold tokens of his grace. There is no study more profitable for the preacher than the study of the lives of saints and martyrs reared in communions outside his own. It breaks down native bigotries and inherited prejudices, and brings the soul to the place in which the astonished Peter found himself when he cried out in the hearing of his incredulous fellow-countrymen who were resisting the admission of the Gentiles into the church, "If then God gave unto them the like gift as he did also unto us, who was I that I could withstand God?" To all the groups of men who have lived and labored in the power of Christ has God granted repentence unto life, and from every denomination can the preacher gather wealth with which to make himself and his people rich.

But better than communing with the souls of men who are in their graves is holding fellowship with men who are now alive. Every preacher should make friends outside of his own denominational household. It tones up the heart to commune with saints of Christian churches far removed in tradition and custom from one's own. Each ecclesiastical discipline imparts a peculiar blessing to those who are subjected to it, which can be communicated in a measure by its possessors to those whom God has educated in a different school. The preacher who is content to know his denominational brethren only, and who has no desire to mingle with those who see the truth from a different angle and express it in a different terminology, robs himself of a means of spiritual culture which, if used, would make him a stronger preacher and a nobler man. Nothing ministers more effectively to the cause of Christian unity than the bringing of clergymen of different denominations together. Denominational isolation breeds suspicion and raises many a spectre in the mind. We are always farthest from the men we know the least. It is easy to say uncharitable things about a body of Christians with not one of whose members we are acquainted. Men who have friends in all denominations never degenerate into bigots, and sometimes become prophets of reconciliation. The preacher must be a man with a friendly heart. He must be the friend of publicans and sinners, and also of saints who do not agree with him in many of his customs and ideas. It is a great thing to be just to those who differ from us in opinion upon matters which we consider momentous, and it is a still greater thing to be generous. To value virtues which are unlike those which our fathers counted cardinal, and to appreciate teachings which have to us an unfamiliar sound, is not easy. To put one's self into the other man's place is in every department of life difficult, probably nowhere more difficult than in the realm of religion. But to do this is a manifest duty of every Christian, and especially of the preacher. The preacher who makes disparaging remarks or ungenerous statements about other branches of the church, or who caricatures their doctrines, forfeits the respect of all right-minded men. A speaker is never under such obligation to be scrupulously correct, down to the last syllable, as when he attempts to state the position of men from whom he differs. If the preacher wishes to controvert the doctrines of another religious body, let him study those doctrines as presented by their ablest exponents, and then state them in the most plausible manner in which it is possible for them to be put. Christian scholars are not fools even if they do not follow after us, and their positions are not to be overturned by a caricature or a jeer, but by an argument framed of reasons which will win the assent of the unprejudiced mind. Controversy is a hazardous and exacting business, and the man who enters it must have clean hands and a pure heart. Useless controversy is always to be avoided, and most pulpit controversies are useless. The controversial preacher is as a rule an unprofitable servant. Even if he keeps his own spirit sweet, he is likely to ruffle the hearts of his hearers. The net result of his labors is ordinarily nothing. Few things are settled by controversy. It is by emphasizing the things upon which all Christians are agreed, rather than by harping upon the things about which they differ, that the divisions of Christendom are to be healed. Each denomination must work out its own salvation, and the best thing which surrounding denominations can do is to hold up a light. Let the preacher attempt to reform his own church family rather than try to set right his neighbors. Sending a chilling gale of criticism against a neighboring church has a tendency to cause it to draw its obnoxious mantle more closely about it. Churches accomplish most when they shine. It is not when they cudgel one another, but when each one goes out with its lamp burning to meet its Lord, that they get rid of their errors, and come closest together.

The church farthest from our Protestant churches is the Roman Catholic, and none, therefore, is better worth our knowing. A Protestant preacher who is not acquainted with the history and doctrines of the Roman Catholic church has been negligent at a point at which carelessness is calamitous. Because of its size, embracing nearly one-half of all the Christians in the world, because of its long history, extending through so many centuries, and because of its present power over the lives of men and nations, it deserves above all other religious organizations to be studied and understood. Both Protestants and Catholics are less informed of each other's doctrines than they ought to be, and it is the ignorance on both sides which is accountable for many things which good men have reason to deplore. The fact that Roman Catholics differ so widely from us at many points renders patient and sympathetic study doubly necessary. It is easy to misunderstand those who are far away. By the haze of distance virtues are often hidden and vices enormously magnified. To understand his Roman Catholic brethren is one of the urgent duties of a Protestant minister. The teachings of Catholicism should be learned from her own authors, undistorted and uncolored by the interpretations of Protestant expositors. We do not hesitate to kindle our spirits at the fire which burns in Augustine's "Confessions," or in Thomas à Kempis' "Imitation of Christ," and we gladly acknowledge our indebtedness to men like Francis of Assisi, and Bernard of Clairvaux. It is also worth one's while to study Roman Catholic histo-

ries, and to master the arguments of the great Roman
Catholic theologians.   But better still than knowing
Roman Catholic books, is knowing living Roman
Catholic men.   There is no substitute for fellowship,
and when Roman Catholic priests and Protestant
ministers come to know one another, the chasm
between the Roman Catholic and Protestant worlds
will be less deep than it is.   It is the separation of the
two sets of men from each other which has perpetuated suspicions and ill-will that ought to have
died long ago.   To many a Protestant the candles
and the incense and the sanctus bell are so foreign,
that the Roman Catholic church seems to belong to
another world.   Between the pomp of the gorgeous
ceremonial before the grand altar, and the unadorned
simplicity of a Protestant order of service, there
appears to be no point in common.   But when devout Protestants and Catholics meet in the fellowship of friendly intercourse they discover that they
are not so far apart as it seemed.   Underneath the
paraphernalia of Roman Catholicism there beats a
great Christian heart, and a Protestant preacher
ought to know it and enter into sympathy with it.
It is a blessing to any Protestant minister to number among his friends a few noble Catholic priests.
Through these friends he will see the whole Catholic

church in a new light, and because of them he will
be less inclined to say bitter things of Roman Catholic errors. That Roman Catholicism has overlaid
the simplicity of the gospel with needless mysteries
and bewildering traditions, and teaches certain doctrines which are erroneous and therefore mischievous, is a fact of which an instructed Protestant has
no doubt.   That some of her practices are dangerous
and some of her emphases overdone, is also a fact
which cannot be hidden.   But there is something
more in Roman Catholicism than error, and all her
actions are not blunders.   In every century she has
given the world scholars, saints, and martyrs, and
while her sins have been crimson, she is not without
achievements of imperishable renown. If she has
not always treated Protestants with mercy or even
justice, our duty to her remains the same. We
are to remember that she is not the only sinner,
and that we too are not free from guilt. If, ecclesi-
astically speaking, she curses us, we are nevertheless
to bless her. If she hates us, we are to pray for
her, and if she persecutes us and despitefully uses
us in all countries in which she has the power, we
are, in all ways which are open, to do good unto her.
To brood over wrongs committed centuries ago, to
feel resentment toward men now living because of

what men did whose bodies have long since been dust, to exploit the moral delinquencies of unworthy men who may officiate at her altars, to coin suspicions into slanders, and convert inferences into wholesale condemnations, this is not worthy of any man who calls himself a Christian, and in Protestant ministers it is monstrous. Wherein the Roman Catholic church is in need of reformation, we can help her most by genuine sympathy and whole-hearted affection and good-will. We cannot refrain from teaching and preaching certain doctrines which are contrary to hers, for to be silent would be to be recreant to the trust which has been given us, and would withhold from her the blessing which we feel sure we are able to impart. But we can hold our tongue from slander, and can keep back our lips from speaking sentences which stab and burn. We can speak the truth in love, and when we differ we can do it in a way which shows unutterable regret. Instead of dwelling upon her failures and her errors, we can meditate occasionally upon the good things which she has long been doing and which she is doing still. We can rejoice that she trains men to worship. It is her glory that she teaches men to kneel. She builds up in human hearts the sense of reverence, and leaves men awestruck and wondering.

The world is indebted to her for bending the human knee. She teaches the principle of obedience. She believes in subordination. These are divine principles which need emphasis, and in building them into the souls of men is she ministering to all mankind. She exalts and glorifies the duty of loyalty to the church. The love of devout Catholics for the church is inexpressibly beautiful. For the church, Catholics will make all sacrifices. Their devotion travels all the way to the gates of death. She has the sense of solidarity and feels the power of the subtle links which bind the generations together. Her saints run backward through the centuries, and she trains men to think of the church as a vast society extended over the earth and sweeping into the heavens, gathering into itself all the affections of the heart, and the entire circle of the interests of mankind. Before the eyes of the devout Roman Catholic the church of God looms sovereign and glorious, the very home and shrine of the Eternal. If we have much to teach her, she has also much to teach us. If she has overemphasized certain principles, we have overemphasized others. If she has overlooked important truths, we also have not been free from dimsightedness. It is a solace and a strength to know that Catholics and Protestants belong together, and that, in spite of our many differences, we are in the depths of our aspirations and hopes one.

Prepare, then, by your preaching the way which shall lead to a reunited church. It doth not yet appear what this church unity shall be, but we know that when it appears it shall have a form which the Lord himself approves. When it shall come no man knows, possibly not even the angels of God. It is not for us to know times and seasons, but power has been promised, and by that power we are to conquer the alienations and separations of Christendom. Every man now entering the ministry ought to ponder the fact that there is a world-wide yearning for Christian unity and also for church union. This is one of the signs of the times which preachers are called to interpret. The Spirit of God is saying something to all of our churches, and it is for the men in the pulpits to train the congregations to listen.

But the reunion of Christendom is not coming in a day, nor as the result of any adroitly devised scheme. The men who rush up and down the world exploiting plausible programs for bringing separated communions together, are not the men who are doing most to put an end to our regrettable divisions. It is not by propositions or compromises that the mighty miracle is to be wrought, but by the baptism of the human heart into a nobler spirit, and a fuller entrance on the part of Christian people into the thought and life of God. Before we have church union we must all go deeper and rise higher. Men say, "Lo, here is a platform upon which we all can stand," or "Lo, there are conditions which we are all able to accept," but he who is wise will not place undue confidence in the promises of the vehement and pushing prophets. Unity is a growth and not a manufactured product. Growths cannot be forced without deranging the processes of life. Forced reunions result in fresh divisions. The churches cannot be welded together by the hammers of our flaming ecclesiastical statesmen. They must be permitted to grow together, for, be it not forgotten, the building upon which preachers are working partakes of the qualities of an edifice and also of a living organism, and no matter how industrious and ingenious the workmen, they are compelled to wait patiently for the completion of the foreordained stages of a development which human ingenuity is unable to hasten or alter. It is a paradox of Christianity that to go fast, one must go slow. In the realm of the spirit the shortest distance between two points is not a straight line. During the last fifty years the churches have been growing together. Much of the bitterness and belligerency has already disappeared. Open hostility has well-nigh ceased in all communities in which the people have emerged from the stone age. In large sections of the Christian world the various communions are at present going their several ways, no longer caring to fight one another, but not quite prepared yet to love one another. We have the quietude of indifference, but not the full-toned harmony of consenting minds. But here and there are signs of a new era. It is daybreak in many lands. The principle of denominational comity is receiving a widening recognition, and coöperation is being extended over larger fields. Federation on a limited scale has already passed from the realm of hope into that of fact, while a few audacious spirits even dare to dream of an organic union that shall take in the entire Protestant world. The young men are seeing visions and the old men are dreaming dreams, and some beautiful thing will some day come to pass. Whatever a preacher may think of the present practicability of organic union, or even of federation, he is under obligation to make the church of which he is the pastor increasingly Christian. He cannot escape the duty of working in season and out of season for a fuller Christian unity. Out of a richer spiritual unity will come, in God's good time, new comities, fresh federations, and amazing organic unions. If he desires church union, then let the preacher develop the spirit of Christian unity. Let him exorcise by his sermons the demons of suspicion, jealousy, bigotry, exclusiveness, and ecclesiastical snobbishness, and endeavor to set his people in the right attitude to all who take upon their lips the blessed name. Let him build up the art of sympathy, the capacity of appreciation, and the principle of coöperation, and give to his church a corporate consciousness, a catholic spirit, a friendly disposition toward all who bow at the name of Jesus. This is foundation work, and a deal of it must still be done before we are prepared to attempt any of those imposing superstructures of church union which tantalize the imagination and set the heart beating. The selfishness of the old individualism runs like a virus in the blood, and the present generation is not prepared for those larger forms of union which, please God, are sure to come. Many a man has wasted his life in pushing things which were premature. It is tragic for men to try to lift the world by ecclesiastical devices to a position which it is the divine will shall be attained only by a steady and silent growth continued through many seasons. The organic union

Q

of all Christian bodies is below the horizon of us who are now living, but the work of promoting spiritual unity is practicable and urgent. In spite of differences in organization and diversities of worship, the branches of the church can be brought closer together in aspiration and endeavor. Congregations can be lifted above the things which divide and alienate. We can plan and lift together. We can join our forces in the work of casting out demons. We can all join in the sacrament of the Basin and Towel. It is impossible to obliterate in the present century all the marks of division, but every one of us can contribute something to the growing unity of the Holy Catholic Church.

Preachers need the inspiration which comes from the vision of the great church to keep their hearts from fainting in the day of battle. It is disastrous to a preacher to have an outlook which is narrowed. Human nature is prone to despondency, and, however optimistic the temperament of the preacher, the down-pulling force of the world's unbelief is sure to leave its mark upon him. The tremendous power of evil grows upon the Christian worker through the years. There is no mystery so deep as the mystery of iniquity, except the mystery of love. A young man, confident in his strength, feels during the earlier years of his ministry that he can successfully cope with this mystery of evil, possibly overcome it. So Elijah felt, and so have all young men felt in the first flush of their initial victories. But as life advances, the battlefield widens, and the warrior begins to see that he is wrestling not against flesh and blood, but against the principalities, against the powers, against the world rulers of this darkness, against the spiritual hosts of wickedness in the heavenly places. It is when the implacable enemy reveals undreamed-of ranges of his infernal and immeasurable strength, that the preacher needs to throw himself back on the doctrine of the Holy Catholic Church. His own little congregation is as nothing in so great a war, his denomination, however large, shrinks into insignificance, a score of Christian communions seem all too few to meet and conquer so formidable a foe. But when he lifts up his eyes and takes in the holy apostolic universal church, with its thundering brigades and wide-flung battle line, and sees how many cohorts of the Lord's soldiers are contending on the wide field, and notes the splendid strength of phalanxes of warriors whose courage and loyalty he had forgotten to count on, and whose very existence had for a time escaped his mind, it is then that he sees Satan falling like lightning from heaven, and enters into the peace of one who has already conquered.

Give yourself horizon. Keep your sky from becoming low. Allow your thought wide ranges. Let your heart roam. Furnish your sympathies spacious room. Look beyond your parish. Take in other parishes. Your parish is the world. Look beyond your denomination. You belong to them all. All things are yours if you are Christ's. Keep alive in your people the consciousness that they belong to a vast multitude whom no man can number. Do not live exclusively in the present. Live also in the past. Look back often to the Reformation, that fiery furnace in which the makers of our modern world walked unharmed, because protected by the presence of the Son of man. Do not stop at the Reformation. Take in with the sweep of your eye the thousand years that preceded Luther, in which God moved in mysterious ways in the work of subjugating barbaric Europe to a gentler temper. Let your glance take in all the epochs of the Christian era, back to the days of the apostles. Link yourself and your church into the chain of life which runs to Golgotha. Never get away from the revelation of God in Christ. Think of the church as an ambassador, treading the highway of the centuries, holding in her keeping the oracles of God, earth's inspired teacher inculcating truths without which the hearts of nations utterly fail, a heaven-sent companion upon whose arm humanity leans as it pursues with bruised, bleeding feet the steep and hazardous way, a vast and ever growing society linking nationalities and races together, the inspirer of music and painting and architecture, the enlightener of men's minds and the searcher of men's hearts, taming the wild ages and curbing the fierce forces, bringing under her dominion every type of genius, and every variety of temper, feeding the souls of heroes and martyrs and saints, and by her glorious ideals and imperishable traditions striking a new unity through a disordered and hopeless world. Let your vision be wide as the earth. Even its full sweeping circumference is not the limit of all that is, for touching it are the clouds of glory which conceal from human eyes the world invisible and the church triumphant. Your church is a part of the family which inhabits the world and the ages, sweeping beyond mortal sight into the upper splendors. In heaven we shall understand, as it is impossible to understand here, the length and breadth and depth of the meaning of the worn and wonderful words: "I believe in the Holy Catholic Church, the communion of Saints."

LECTURE VII

BUILDING THE PLAN

BUILDING THE PLAN

IF a cardinal condition of success in the Christian ministry is an unclouded vision of the thing to be done, a second essential is the formulation of a plan by which the work shall be accomplished. First, the vision of the goal, then the method of reaching it. There are two classes of ministers whose careers are tragic. The first are those who see not clearly what it is they are to do. The world for them lies shrouded in a mist. They walk like men in a fog. The second see with some degree of clearness the destination, but they are too careless or precipitate to build the agencies by which the goal can be attained. Both classes of men arrive nowhere, the first because they do not know where they want to go, the second because they lack the wisdom of fitting means to ends.

If we think of the Christian minister as a builder, the necessity of planning presses itself at once upon the mind. What is an architect but a designer, and what is a builder but a man who makes and follows plans? Before a pencil is put to paper, the architect sees the building which is to be ; and before the first shovel of earth is turned for the foundation, specifications have been accurately and voluminously elaborated. Builders never dash ahead, not knowing whither they are going. The planning intellect has gone before them, carefully marking out the way. The depth and thickness of the foundations, the length and composition of all the walls, the dimensions of every chamber, the location of every door and window, the position of every pipe and wire and chimney, a thousand details are thought out and fixed before the stones are blasted from the quarry or the first load of lumber is ordered from the mill. It is not the way of builders to plunge blindly into their work, trusting to the inspiration of the moment or some happy conjunction of events to guide them in the shaping of the structure for which the world is waiting. Doors and windows cannot be located at the dictate of a passing fancy, nor can the proportions of an edifice which is to delight the eyes and serve the needs of many generations be left to the caprice of men who have started with no definite conception of how the different parts of the building are to be organized into a well-balanced and serviceable whole. When men dedicate themselves to the construction of a cathedral, months, and it may be years, are devoted to the perfecting of the plan. The voids are spaced, the solids are proportioned, the contours are traced. There is a central idea, and everything develops from something else. It is only by painstaking planning that the proportions are at last made perfect, and the arrangement becomes so natural that it seems to be inevitable. Preaching is a science and an art. Preachers are architects and artists. Men are living stones to be built into a growing temple. They who work upon this temple must understand and obey the subtle and inexorable laws of spiritual architecture. They must restrain caprice. They must work with a firm and steady hand, the hand made steady by a far-seeing eye. The eye must see what ought to be, and trace the lines of what is to be, and all the preacher's toil must be coöperant to an end.

The man who is called to the work of church building ought to study and practise the art of planning. The plan itself is a sort of edifice to be built by patient thought and conscientious care. It is not a waste of time to give hours and days to the work of pondering and maturing schedules for future operations. Each day should be surveyed from the vantage point of its earliest working hour, each week should be mapped before its first day has reached its noon, each month should be laid out before it has arrived. The preacher should work upon his plan continually, modifying it from time to time in obedience to the movements of the divine spirit, perfecting it in the illumination of the increasing light. His plan is an invisible temple in whose construction the sound of hammers is never heard, but which, though a purely spiritual creation, and known to God and the preacher only, is a potent factor in giving shape and beauty to the temple built of flesh and blood which is to stand before the world.

The best of all times for the work of planning is a minister's vacation. This is one of the two best uses to which a vacation can be put. The first object of a vacation is relaxation. The bow which is always bent deteriorates in value as a weapon. The field from which the same crop is year after year demanded, after a while runs out. The brain is like the soil and must be given seasons to lie fallow. No mind can give out perpetually. There must be extended periods for receiving. The largest reservoir in time becomes empty if a constant stream flows out and no compensating stream flows in. When ministers cross the deadline at fifty, it is because they have been lazy, or because they have worked so continuously as to fag the

brain. When the mental field is exhausted, the
sermonic crops are thin, and the saints begin to say
of the man in the pulpit, "He is a good man, but he
cannot preach."   In some cases it is the saints which
are largely responsible for this tragic ending of a
minister's career.   Because of their ignorance they
allowed their pastor no sufficient vacation, and by
holding him unbrokenly to his task, they killed his
mind.   And they also wore out his heart.   His heart
became fatigued, and he could not bring to his work
the elasticity and spring of a healthy spirit, or infuse
into his sermons the freshness of a soul which has
retained its buoyancy and sparkle.   A preacher is a
catapult.   He is always hurling things, ideas, arguments, exhortations, expositions.   To accomplish
his ends he must project himself.   His office compels
him to throw his soul upon the souls of others.
But this work, if continued through too long a
stretch, is hurtful to the man who does it, and may
prove fatal to him.   A man cannot be a catapult all
the time.   The expulsive muscles of the mind must
be given respite.   The receptive faculties must have
opportunity to grow and gather stores.   The minister must at times sit down.   He must let others feed
him.   Like the Man of Men, he must go apart into a
desert place and rest awhile.   This is his duty.   He

shirks it at his peril. Every minister should have
at least one month out of every twelve for relaxation. If the parish is large, two months are better
than one. In any case, two weeks is no vacation at
all. One week is required for clearing out the mind
so that the minister is able to rest, and the second
week loses its healing virtue if broken into by preparation for the sermons for the first Sunday after
his return. Nothing less than a month deserves
the name of vacation for a preacher. If church
officials are unwilling to grant one month in twelve,
they should be instructed. Men who mean well
often crucify God's servants, not knowing what
they do. Pastorates must of necessity be short,
if ministers are not given reasonable spaces for
recuperation. It should be the ambition of every
church and all pastors to make the pastorate
long.

It is when the minister is not driven by the duties
of the ordinary days that he can best plan for the
work of the coming year. One can see his church
best when he gets away from it. Detachment supplies the eyes with new lenses. An artist working
in oil steps back again and again from the canvas
in order to see what he is doing. The minister
should every year stand back from his church, and

examine it in the light of a changed perspective. At his leisure he can observe how far the development of his ideal has progressed, and may possibly discover defects which had escaped his notice. He will find that certain things have gotten out of their true relations, and certain other things do not exist in correct proportions. The shadows are too intense, the high lights are not strong enough. The emphasis has been too insistent at certain points, and there are drifts and tendencies which need immediate attention. Many a valley must be exalted, and several hills must be brought low in order that the way of the Lord may be prepared. A careful survey of the last year's work is an excellent discipline for fitting one to plan intelligently for the year to come. A wise minister is never idle on his vacation. There are a hundred things which he can attend to while he is sitting down. He can mend his nets. They have become worn and possibly torn by the hard usage of the year, and he can now look them over and repair them. Certain methods have proved faulty, and these can be investigated and improved. What is the church itself but a big net let down into the human sea? It is always getting torn, and the minister on his vacation can leisurely examine the rents. He can deal with his church as a physician treats a patient, making a careful diagnosis, ascertaining the weak spots in the organism, and deciding on certain courses of treatment which promise to bring the invalid into fuller health.   He can look the church over as a teacher surveys his school, asking himself what are the pupils' chief defects, and what are the graces to which most thought and time should be devoted in order to bring the school up to the standard prescribed by the Great Teacher.   He can inspect his church as a general sizes up his army, counting up the troops which are available for action, making a roll of those who are in the hospital unable to bear the shock of battle, or even the fatigue of the march. He can mentally reconnoitre the country of the enemy, studying his position, pondering his resources, speculating as to his probable powers of resistance, and calculating the chances of a victorious attack.   He can scrutinize his church as a builder runs his eyes up and down a building, noting the cracks and stains, measuring the extent of the dilapidation which time and wear have wrought, and devising plans for its cleansing and complete restoration.   A minister ought to come back from his vacation knowing what he is going to do.   If, in the quiet hours of his holiday, he has on mountain side, or by the sea, or under some ancient oak or pine, or on the waters of some lovely lake, looked at his church with eyes made keen by love, and has made mental note of its deficiencies and delinquencies, and has catalogued its opportunities and immediate obligations, and if he has meditated on the difficulties of the situation, and weighed the obstacles which must be overcome, and if he has balanced in his mind the comparative merits of different plans of campaign, and has decided which one gives largest promise of success, he will carry in his soul an inspiration which will communicate itself to his people, and will find himself endowed with a strength and courage which will lighten the heaviest burdens and throw round the most desperate enterprises the halo of hopefulness. A church likes to feel itself in the grip of a man who knows where he is going. Nothing is so discouraging to Christian people as to feel that their leader is not leading. The outlook is indeed dark if the preacher does not know what things he and his church ought to bring to pass. Simply to keep the church machinery running for the sake of seeing the wheels go round, is a vexation of spirit, driving church members into the mood of the man who exclaimed: "Vanity of vanities, all is vanity." A minister has not made the highest

R

possible use of his vacation unless he comes out of it with a plan for the next year's work.

The benefits of a plan are manifold. It helps the minister save his soul. It protects him against the encroachments of all sorts of idle and thoughtless people who are ready to eat up a minister's strength and time. A man who has not had actual experience in the Christian ministry has not the faintest conception of the pressure, constant and tremendous, to which a pastor is subjected. His tasks are multitudinous, and he is in peril of being dissipated and broken by them. When one has too many things to do, he becomes bewildered and helpless. The young preacher is likely to be pushed hither and thither by people and events, until the week becomes a turmoil and a tangle. Driven by forces which are as pitiless as furies, he feels sometimes like a straw blown about by the parish wind. His good intentions are smashed to splinters by the impact of chance happenings. The world is full of good-hearted but inconsiderate people, amiable, but cruel because they do not think. Men who have no connection with the church rush to the minister when they have axes to grind. He is asked to do a hundred things which he ought not to attempt to do. The ministry has in it many exhausted men who

have frittered away their energies on a multitude
of unrelated errands and bootless projects.   Caught
in this seething whirlpool of parochial activity,
the preacher suddenly finds himself face to face with
a new Lord's day calling for two sermons which he
has had no time to prepare.   He goes into the pulpit
shamefaced, knowing that his message is not related
to the message that preceded it, or to the message
which is likely to come after it, but is a haphazard
thing extemporized to meet the emergency of an
embarrassing occasion.   A man who works in this
fashion is not an artist.   He is a clodhopper.   He
is living from hand to mouth and therefore belongs
to the shiftless and defective classes.   The church of
such a minister will be an unshapely, ungainly thing,
and as soon as possible he will exchange it for another.

A definite and well-considered plan is a minister's life preserver.   It helps him to hold the outside world in its place, and to keep his parish from
crushing him.   A good-natured man, unless he is
shielded by a plan, is apt to be wheedled into all
sorts of useless undertakings and inveigled into
many kinds of intellectual and social dissipation.
The minister is indeed the servant of all, but this
does not mean that he is to be the drudge of every

little despot who crosses his path and beckons to him. He is the servant of all, and therefore cannot allow himself to be undone by a foolish few. A preacher should plan his study hours, and hedge them in with a wall of fire. He should plan his social life, and keep himself rigorously within the bounds which his own good sense has circumscribed. He should live within his income. Are there not twelve hours in the day, and has not the stock of nervous energy also its limitations? A man cannot do everything he would like to do, or everything which other people want him to do, or everything which the world tells him he ought to do. He must pick and choose the particular things which he is convinced God wants him to do, and when undiscerning and meddlesome people urge him to do this and that and beg him to go here and there, let him think of the Man who never once allowed himself to be elbowed from his path, calmly saying, "My hour is not yet come."

A plan saves the minister from the tyranny of his own moods and caprices. Most preachers have moods in abundance, and of luxuriant variety. Inspirational men are exceptionally sensitive, and responsive to their environment. It is because they can be moved that they are able to move others.

Coarse-grained and stolid men never make inspiring preachers. The temperament which fits a man to become the medium of the spirit of life is specially susceptible to wayward inspirations and depressing humors. The preacher, more than most men, fluctuates in the tone of his feelings. He is up and down, exalted and abased, in heaven and not in heaven. Like Elijah he is jubilant to-day on Carmel, and to-morrow he is under the Juniper tree. This week he has the best church in the world, next week he is meditating the paragraphs of his letter of resignation. These elations and depressions are psychological experiences with which ministers, with few exceptions, are compelled to contend. It is well to plan for them in order that they may not work havoc. Many a minister in a despondent mood has taken a step which has filled years with regret. No man is himself in his depleted hours. The judgment gets twisted when the fires of life burn low. Virtue is going out of a minister all the time, because some one is always touching him. The drain of the blood of the nerves is constant. He should save himself from himself by a plan. A plan is a bulwark against aberrations. Every man has his luminous hours, and a plan formed in the light can be carried out through hours of gloom. The path which one has seen from the mountain can be followed even after it has been blurred by the inblowing mist. A plan is a bridge which carries the preacher over rushing torrents of dark feeling, an angel which protects him through the storm of the wild night. The soul of a preacher is not secure without a plan.

It is by planning that a minister also escapes from the clutches of the demon of indefiniteness. Vagueness of expression, vagueness of thought, vagueness of policy, these constitute a trinity of demons which the preacher must at all costs overcome. Demons do not like plans. They are all opposed to order, for order is heaven's first law. They are the friends of confusion, the makers of chaos. If a preacher can be induced to follow his impulses and to rely on his fitful enthusiasms, the infernal world rejoices. It is the man who sits down and counts the cost of the tower who is most likely to finish it. It is the general who carefully calculates the resources both of himself and of his enemy who increases his chances of winning the victory. The successful preacher is the man who first of all takes time to ascertain precisely what it is he wants to do, and then takes additional time for working out his plan of doing it. When a preacher preaches, and men go home from the sermon not knowing what the preacher was trying to accomplish, and when he works an entire year among his people and leaves them at the end of the year in doubt as to what he wanted them to do and be, he is a workman of whom the church of God has reason to be ashamed. The preacher ought to work upon his plan in order to sharpen his mind. He can dissipate a fog by creating a program. It is only by building a good plan that he can save himself from the humiliation of making a botch of his church.

For the sake also of the people the minister ought to plan his work. It is a wonderful liberty which is granted to ministers, and the liberty ought to be used humbly and in the fear of God. To them is given the privilege of determining not only what hymns shall be sung, what truths shall be unfolded, what duties enforced, what warnings shall be sounded, what consolations administered, but also, except in liturgical churches, what Scripture shall be read, and what shall be the length and character of all the prayers. The whole ordering, not only of public worship, but of parochial activity, is left practically in their hands. It is a heavy responsibility not always appreciated, a solemn trust which is oftentimes abused. If the minister does not plan

his work, his people are at the mercy of his impulses
and fancies, his prejudices and idiosyncrasies, possibly his vagaries and hallucinations. He will, unless he guards himself against it, follow his natural
likings, choosing always the line of least resistance,
and thus he will give his people not what they ought
to have, but what it happens to be easiest for him to
give. In this way he will fall into ruts and even
gullies, dragging all his unhappy flock with him.
His instruction will lack balance. The life of
the parish will languish, struck through with the
deadening monotone of a selfish man. The impulses
of the passing hour are poor guides in the realm of
ministerial duty. The preacher must use his reason.
He should present to God and his parish a reasonable service. Having looked backward and forward
and all around, he should lay out his work on a
rational basis, with due consideration to all the
different interests which have a right to be recognized. A plan drawn by the reason tugs at a man
and pulls him in spite of his biases and preferences
into wider orbits. The man who plans for his people
crucifies many of his own fancies and foibles. The
human heart, even in the breast of a preacher,
is deceitful above all things, and it is desperately
sick. The deceitfulness can be in a measure cir-

cumvented by a plan. Who has not seen a minister riding proudly down the Appian Way of his own tastes and ambitions, dragging his parish at his chariot wheels? But if the church be the bride of Christ, it is she who is in the chariot, and the preacher is her servant. She is reading the book of Life, and like the Ethiopian eunuch whom Philip overtook, she is perplexed by certain paragraphs and phrases. It is for the preacher to draw near, find the enigmatic passages, and proceed to their systematic unfolding and orderly application. In building his plan the preacher keeps his eye on his church. When a minister acts off-hand, without pre-meditation, he may forget to act like a Christian; but when he sits down and calmly forecasts the year, he is certain, unless he be a son of perdition, to look not only on his own things but also on the things of others. Planning for his people reduces the self-ishness of the preacher's heart. Paul was a father, a mother, and a brother to his converts. He was always anticipating their wants, making some new provision for their souls.

For the sake of himself and his people every minister ought to have a church year. If he is not the servant of a communion which supplies him with a schedule ready made, let him make one for himself. He can make a better one, possibly, than can any ecclesiastical council, however august. The unanswerable objection against all calendars devised for the use of Christian bodies is that they are too stiff. Not enough room is allowed for the free play of the life of the individual churches. Wide liberty is needed in the planning of public worship, and great flexibility is desirable in the framework of the plan. The church of God exists in different zones, and therefore in different climates; and consequently the almanac is not a safe guide-book for the church in the work of planning its worship. Races differ greatly in temperament and culture, communities differ widely in tradition and social custom. To try to force all churches into a common temporal schedule irritates and fetters. The church that uses in all its congregations a table of Scripture readings made out by men who lived three hundred years ago needlessly hampers its ministers in the doing of their work. The appointed lesson for the day is often inappropriate, either because of the character of the congregation, or the season of the year, or the overshadowing of some great and recent event which calls for Scripture of a different tone. To have the same theme treated in all churches on the same day is striving after a uniformity which is not worth what it costs. The interests of the local congregation should be jealously safeguarded, and every pastor ought to be granted large freedom in shaping the worship to the particular requirements of his own parish. For instance, the descent of the Holy Spirit is an event which, along with the birth of Jesus and his resurrection, ought to be commemorated every year, but there is no compelling reason why the coming of the Spirit should be celebrated only on the seventh Sunday after Easter. For Easter is itself a movable festival, it being impossible to hold fast to the precise anniversary day of Jesus' rising from the tomb. The dates in the almanac are such formal and flimsy things that there is no necessity for binding to any one of them inseparably any one of the great events in the life of our Lord. If the larger part of a minister's congregation do not remain in the city seven weeks after Easter, why should he not preach his Pentecostal sermon on some earlier Sunday? To keep the correct sequence of the events is desirable, but to observe the precise day is not important.

Several centuries ago the non-conformist bodies of Great Britain threw away the traditional ecclesiastical year, and for reason. The church calendar had become a part of the yoke which it was impossible longer to bear. It was freighted with associations which were disturbing to many consciences and hearts. The number of festivals and fasts, of vigils and feasts, of bishops, martyrs, confessors, and saints to be commemorated, had been so multiplied that the church calendar had become a burden and scandal. But the idea which lies at the root of the church year is a sound one, and there is no reason why all ministers, no matter what their ecclesiastical connections, should not make use of it. The root idea is that the fundamental facts and truths of the Christian religion shall be commemorated at stated times every year. Such an annual commemoration has many things to commend it. It is helpful to the minister in that it keeps him from wandering away from the things which he is ordained to proclaim. It safeguards the church against the neglect of vital Christian doctrine. It fosters the natural growth of the spiritual life. If a minister marks upon his calendar at the beginning of the year the cardinal events in the life of Jesus, and the foundation doctrines of the Christian faith, he will save himself from a variety which is distracting, and from a monotony which is benumbing, and his people from that ignorance of evangelic truth which lies like a blight upon so many congregations. There are certain themes of such moment to the soul that the preacher should deal with them every year. The sovereignty of God, the love of God, the birth and death and resurrection and character of Jesus, the work of the Holy Spirit, the Great Commandment, the New Commandment, and the Golden Rule, faith and hope and love, prayer, Bible study, and self-sacrificing service, the guilt and penalty of sin, the call to repentance, the offer of forgiveness, civic duty, international peace, missions at home and abroad, the communion of saints, and the life eternal, — surely no year would be complete with any of these sovereign themes omitted. They are themes which never grow old. They can never be exhausted. They are springs at which our fathers drank, and the last generation which shall live upon this earth will find refreshment in them. There are at least twenty themes on which a minister ought to preach every year. They are the old things which he is to bring out of his treasury again and again, giving them each year a different body, and pouring into them each year a fresh passion which will make them all new.

Still other sermons can be decided on before the year opens. These will be upon themes which were not touched upon last year and which need not be repeated in the year which is to follow. Truth is a vast country, and there is no reason why a preacher should settle down in one small corner of it. It should be his ambition each succeeding year to conduct his hearers into at least one new region of the Scriptures, in which the scenery is somewhat unfamiliar, and where the flowers and fruits expand one's conception of the lovely and luscious things which grow in the garden of the Lord. Many of these sermons can be coördinated. They can be organized into groups or courses. Sermons can be trained to help one another. They are not Christian sermons if they recognize no neighbors and confess no duties. They ought to march like soldiers enlisted for a great campaign. The sermons which come late ought to support the sermons which came early, and carry onward the work which they began. There ought to be a spiritual unity running through the year, and one increasing purpose. What these sermons ought to be, the preacher cannot tell until he has made a careful study of the spiritual condition of his church. What does it lack? Faith, cheerfulness, hopefulness, patience, aggressiveness, reverence, love? Whatever it lacks the sermons ought to supply. A preacher ought to be as wise as a farmer. A farmer decides what crops he wants, and selects his seeds accordingly. He knows he will reap what he sows. The preacher has the advantage of the farmer in that the preacher can not only select his seeds, but he can also control the weather. He can determine the quantity of the sun and the dew. He can fix the sequence of the seasons. If he does not get the fruit he desires, it is because he does not understand the creation and management of spiritual meteorological conditions.

The skilled preacher ever works to make an impression. Deep impressions are made by concentrating forces upon definite points. If sermons are entirely disconnected, and if one sermon does not care what sermon preceded it, or what sermon is going to follow, the best results are impossible. One reason why the noises of the street weary us is because there is no unity running through them. They are disconnected and therefore discordant. The tones of a symphony soothe and charm because in the variety of tones there lives a unity. By concentration the composer produces a mighty effect. The sermons of a year ought to be a symphony. A few dominant notes should be carried through all the music of the year, other notes being held in subordination, and yet even these subordinate parts not being neglected, but organized and compelled to contribute to the harmonious whole. The architectonic genius of a man comes out in building his course of instruction for a year.

It is of great advantage to a preacher to carry in his eye a score of dates on which sermons on particular themes are to fall due. By fixing the dates long in advance and compelling the mind to fall in with the predetermined schedule, the minister gains self-mastery, and escapes from the intolerable bondage of an intellect dependent on moods. It is a great thing to be delivered from the crotchets of a reluctant and recalcitrant mind. After a while the mind comes to like this orderly procedure, and goes to work with enthusiasm when the appointed hour strikes. Men who carry sermon themes long in their mind are always surprised by the ease with which the sermons, when called for, come forth. The mind has queer ways of working below consciousness, and a theme once given to it is probably unfolding day after day, although we ourselves are unconscious of its growth. One never knows what is going to happen when he puts a truth to soak in the juices of the mind. The mind is a capacious receptacle and one can put twenty themes into it as well as one, and all the twenty will have room in which to develop. Put twenty subjects into the mind at the beginning of the year, and no matter what book you open, sentences will fly out of the book, and light on one or another member of this group of themes, just as bees when let loose in a field light on the flower which contains the nectar which they most relish. Or, to change the figure, build your arbor at the beginning of the year, set out your vines, and they will grow day and night, you know not how, for God will nourish them in ways known only to himself, and you will have in every season abundant fruit for the nourishment of your people.

It is desirable that the Scripture lessons for the service of public worship should also be planned. Their selection certainly ought not to be left to accident or caprice. The man who reads to his people the first chapter that happens to occur to him, is related to the man who preaches a sermon on the first text on which his eye happens to alight. They are both brothers of the primitive medicine man. Luck has no place in the Christian pulpit. Everything should be done decently and in order, nothing at random or haphazard. The public reading of the Scriptures is a part of the educational system of the Christian church, and the work ought to be carried on with premeditation and a clear-eyed, comprehen-

s

sive purpose. If a minister follows his own inclinations, he is likely to read and reread his favorite chapters. If he always reads the chapter which chances to contain his text, he will deprive his people of many chapters which deserve a place in the worship of the church. There was a book of Scripture which was lost once by the clergymen of the Jewish church, and, strange to say, it was lost in the temple. In many a Christian church more than one book of the Bible is lost. Its message is never heard in public worship. Even ministers who entertain exalted theories of inspiration sometimes have a curious fashion of treating whole books of Holy Writ as though they were books of straw. They do not ostracize these books intentionally, but drop them because there is no method in their church administration. Unless a preacher plans to travel systematically through the Bible in the worship of the church, he will unconsciously come back repeatedly to a few chapters which are congenial because they are familiar. It is unwise for a man to make his own taste dictator in deciding what Scriptures shall be read. Many men have many minds and many needs and many tastes, and the Bible is a myriad-sided book intended for a myriad-sided humanity. Because a Bible book does not appeal to the preacher is no sufficient reason for exiling it from the Christian pulpit. Its lack of appeal may be due to the fact that the preacher has outgrown it, or that he has not yet grown up to it. Saints in the pew, maturer than he is, might feed upon it with thanksgiving, or immature disciples might find in it the simple food which children need. The preacher who ignores the Old Testament in his Scripture reading because the New Testament is higher, robs and wrongs his people. The Old Testament was the only Bible of our Lord. It is the book which the apostles kept open before them while they preached. It is the book which passed like iron into the blood of the Puritans, making them strong to overthrow ancient tyrannies and establish the world on a new foundation. There is ethical instruction in the Old Testament which will never be outgrown. In the regeneration of modern society and the creation of a new world order, the prophets of Israel have a great rôle to play. There is no book in the Bible which the modern church does not need. Many chapters, to be sure, deal with things transitory and local, and have no claim upon the modern church in her worship or life, but the Bible as a whole, and not the Bible in fragments or fractions, is a book to be given to the people.

The planning of Scripture readings brings blessings

to the preacher. It carries him into regions into which, if left to his own impulses, he might never go. Even in Bible regions which seem to be nothing but rock and sand, he will find precious material for the building of the church. The steady, progressive movement of pastor and people across the entire Bible world introduces a variety into the Sunday service which breaks the monotony of the pulpit ministrations. If the preacher is a narrow man, lacking in versatility and range, and preaches sermons of but a single type, a relief is given to the service by introducing into it the varied voices of a great company of men who by divers portions and in divers manners proclaim the character and will of God. Every preacher, no matter how talented, needs all available weapons for the slaying of that arch enemy of all preachers — Monotony. Various lectionaries — tables of Bible lessons — have been prepared by various branches of the Christian church, but none of them is, in my judgment, satisfactory. Why should not the preacher make his own? Let him go carefully through the Bible, culling out the chapters which contain either milk or meat for the present generation, and let these selected passages be arranged in an ordered sequence, which can be travelled through in at least five years. The building of this lectionary is one of the first pieces of constructive work to which the young preacher may wisely devote not a few of his leisure hours.

If a minister plans his Scripture lessons for five years, why not other things? We are never at our best unless we are working for results too great to be attained in a single year. The lines of action must be long if the pulse is to be even, and the endeavor steady. A long pastorate is to be craved and planned for. A minister on taking charge of a parish ought to lay out his work on the supposition that he will remain where he is at least five years. He may, it is true, not remain a year. Any one of many conceivable combinations of circumstances may render an extended pastorate inadvisable or impossible, but no man should allow contingencies to dictate the planning of his life. In a world like this all things are possible. The preacher may die next year, next month, next week, to-night, but no sensible man allows possibilities a chief place in determining what he is going to aim to do. Some things must be assumed, and one of them is that the man is going to live and that his pastorate will not be short. A minister who expects to die next week cannot do his best work, neither can a man who expects to change his parish next year. If with the eye of faith he sees the years stretching out before him, he can work with a clearer eye and grip the world with a steadier hand. He will possess that which is indispensable to a successful teacher, — a quiet heart. Men who are restless and wavering, always anticipating a change, never succeed as preachers. The feeling of unsettledness burns like a fever in the blood, consuming the vital elements of strength. With a long pastorate in his eye a minister is less likely to do shoddy work. He will not cultivate those mushroom growths which flourish and wilt like Jonah's gourd. The parish will not be made feverish by being placed under high pressure methods. The new pastor will not go at things furiously, as some young men do, striking a pace which it is impossible for any mortal to keep up, but he will swing into a steady gait which can be maintained through the years. The difficult thing in the ministry is not to fly for a spell like an eagle, or to run for a season like a race horse, but to walk a long time and not faint.

With five possible years before him a man has encouragement to formulate a plan. Men do not lay long plans who expect to leave their church at the end of a few months. It is not human nature to set out trees whose fruit one never expects to eat, to make sacrifices for a cause whose prosperity one never expects to see, to prepare for triumphs which one has no hope of enjoying. A man who expects a short pastorate has many inducements to do surface work. He is tempted to do only those things which make a show. The deep and difficult things will be passed by. Such a man dwarfs himself and blights the parish. If the preacher feels that he is only a transient guest in the ecclesiastical inn, waiting for the next train to carry him to a more commodious hotel, all his people will know it and no one will have heart to do the things which cost blood. Fidgety men ought never to go into the ministry. Nomads are out of place in the realm of pastoral service. Men who become the pastor of a church simply to use its pulpit as a stepping-stone to something higher, ought to be outlawed by all churches. When a minister consents to become the pastor of a church let him settle down, resolved never to leave it until it is made clear that his work there has been carried to such a point that he can in justice to the great church of God pass on to a field which calls for still harder service.

A man can build great plans if he has several years over which to stretch them. He can lay out courses of study for his own intellectual development, and by his plan he will save himself from squandering his

time on the miscellaneous books which the pub-
lishers thrust on him, or which his parishioners ask
him to read. Many a minister has been wrecked by
reading without purpose and method. He had no
plan of his own, and so he was at the mercy of every
one who volunteered a suggestion. He can also plan
his studies in theology, history, biography, and
poetry, four branches indispensable to a man who
wishes to be a master-teacher of men. Certain subjects will be assigned to each of the years, and certain
volumes will be set apart for each of the months,
and no sort of conspiracy on the part of men or
devils will be allowed to break down the minister's
determination to pursue the prearranged course to its
end. Desultory reading and spasmodic study have
slain their thousands. A man who forms a clean-cut
plan and clings to it heroically through the opposi-
tions of the years, is a man who advances in wisdom
and stature, and in favor with God and men.

Even the sermons can be planned for a period of
five years — not all of them, but those which deal with
truths which come up every year for fresh treatment.
A man can plan five sermons on the doctrine of God,
or the character of Jesus, or the work of the Holy
Spirit, or the Christian church, or the Life Eternal,
or Missionary Work and Workers, each sermon ap-

proaching the subject by a different route, and viewing it from a different standpoint. Unless a preacher plans his annually recurring sermons, he will find himself saying the same things every year, and his people, wondering why the sermons are so tedious, will make no progress in their apprehension of these cardinal themes. By cutting a great truth into sections, and assigning one section to each year, the preacher will at the end of a term of years have the joy of knowing that he himself has made progress in the mastery of truth, and that his people are in possession of a wider and wealthier kingdom.

After a minister has served an apprenticeship in laying five-year plans, he may venture upon the work of planning for ten years. Having learned how to map out the work of ten years, he will be ready to plan the remainder of his life. He cannot plan it in detail, but the outlines can be sketched, and these can be filled in as the needed light is furnished. No man's plan can be carried out entirely as he framed it, for we are under the government of a God who also makes plans, and when our plans conflict with His plans, it is our plans which are broken. But, using the light we have, we should project long courses of action, and when another girds us and we are carried whither we would not go, it is our con-

solation to know we are in the hands of One who
plans only for our good. Paul planned to go into
Bithynia, but his plan was shattered. He purposed
to enter a province, and God gave him a continent.
While we are weeping over our failure to enter Bithynia, we are in fact on our way to Troas, where a
new vision awaits us, and larger fields are to be opened
to us by the generosity of the incomprehensible,
wonder-working God.

It is a good thing for a preacher to look often down
the years which slope toward the sunset, and see himself as he would like' himself to be at the end of the
day. It is good also to behold in a dream the
Church of God rising in the distance, glorious with
the proportions and graces which it ought to have,
if all the builders do their duty. Occasionally one
should picture himself in that bright world where,
the fires of judgment having done their work, it shall
be made evident how much of the material which
the preacher used was hay and wood and stubble. It
is when the eyes are cleansed by the touch of the
upper worlds that we see the emptiness of reputation,
the hollowness of cheap successes, and realize the
transitoriness of the pride of place and the pomp of
learning. In our Patmos hours it is revealed to us
that it is not our predecessors toward whom our

eyes should most frequently be turned, but toward our successors, the men who are to labor after we are in our graves. It is not for us to strive to equal or surpass the men who have gone before us, but so to work as to make it easier for the men who come after us to bring the church to a new perfection. We stand in the line of a great succession, and to so link ourselves to the men behind, and the men before, as to enable God to do through us the work for which we were created — this is victory.

The first great preacher had but one ambition, to apprehend that for which also he was apprehended by Christ Jesus. Can any heart soar to a loftier height? Paul planned his work. He left nothing to caprice. He did not run uncertainly. He did not fight as one who beats the air. He had a burning purpose and a shining goal, and he pressed on steadily toward the mark. It is a thrilling shout of victory, his exultant cry, "I have finished the course."

Jesus of Nazareth planned his work. In communion with his Father he fashioned his course patiently through the years. He had a cup to drink, and a baptism to be baptized with, and he was straitened until it was accomplished. There is a rapture in his confession to his Father, "I have accomplished the work which thou hast given me to do."

His joy on earth reached its climax in the exclamation of his latest hour, "It is finished!" When a man gives himself to the work of preaching, holding back nothing, giving all, when he plans his life and work with an eye single to God's glory, ever aiming to bring his plan into deepening harmony with the plan of Heaven, he becomes a successor of the apostles, and enters into the joy of his Lord.

LECTURE VIII

THE BUILDING OF THE BUILDER

THE BUILDING OF THE BUILDER

Two queries have no doubt arisen in many an alert mind while we have been walking together along the way: Why has there been no lecture on the "Building of the Sermon"? and why has the "Building of the Builder" been relegated to the closing hour? In all building operations does not the Builder come first? Does not the plan proceed from him? Does not the edifice depend on him? Is he not the first link in the chain, the fountain from which all else proceeds? Why not build the preacher, and then proceed to build the church?

The preacher comes last in this course of lectures, because in the work of building he comes first. It is a paradox of Christianity that those who are first are often last. He who would find himself must lose himself, and only to him who makes himself of no reputation and lays down his life, is the promise given. It was the Master's way to set men, first of all, not face to face with themselves, but face to face with their task, and it was by the patient doing of their task that they were to save their souls.

Many things he was wont to tell them about the importance and difficulty of the work to which he had called them, and few things apparently did he say about their own salvation.   They were to seek first of all the Kingdom of God, to build a brotherhood in which the love of God should be controlling and by which the will of God should get itself done on earth, and, doing this, they would find all necessary things being added.   The apostles were men, and therefore interested in their own personal advancement, but whenever they attempted to induce Jesus to speak of their own dignities and promotions, he began to talk again about their work.   Even up to the edge of the ascension cloud they carried their discussions of rank and dominion, but to the end the only assurance which was given to them was that they should have sufficient strength with which to do their work. He left them face to face with a church that was to be built, and it was in the building of this church that they were to grow into that fulness of stature which is appointed for the sons of God.

Many of the tragedies of the Christian ministry are caused by the minister getting into the wrong place.   Everything seems to conspire to push him to the front.   His own native inclinations and ambitions, the love of place, the love of praise, and the love of power, render the first place attractive, and all the kingdoms of the world outside of him are in league with the world inside of him, to keep the eyes of the minister upon himself. When he comes to the seminary, he is taken in charge by a group of experts whose business it is to call his attention to himself. One man lays hold upon his voice, and asks him to study it, to note its intonations, inflections, cadences, to observe his gestures and keep track of them. Another selects his diction, and requests him to criticise it, to keep his eye on his adjectives, his relative pronouns, and the structure of his sentences. Another takes his sermons and bids him take them to pieces and study each separate part, inspecting it under the microscope of the critical judgment. Another collects his doctrinal beliefs, his conceptions of God and man, the Scriptures and the Sacraments, and rivets his gaze upon them, requesting him to sit in judgment on them, to pry into their origin, to analyze them and to find reasons for them. It may be that some one will even dig up the roots of his "call to the ministry." All young men come out of the seminary more or less introspective and self-conscious. It is inevitable.

The process begun in the seminary is carried on by the parish. A minister's task drags him to the

T

front. He cannot do his work in a corner. He must have the uppermost room. At every feast he is at the head of the table. He is the observed of all observers. He must be not only seen but heard. He must always be speaking or praying or reading. He cannot help displaying his gifts. This exhibition of himself invites criticism. If he is handsome, he will overhear some one remarking it. If he has a good voice, many will tell him so. If his style is effective, the compliments will be abundant. If his success is conspicuous, the silver bugles will blow a musical blast across the town. His name will be on many lips, and the light of many rejoicing eyes will illumine his triumphant way. A man cannot hear the band playing in his honor without thinking of himself. No matter how humble, he is likely to become self-conscious in the major key. The building of himself is suggested to him, not by demons but by the saints, and the building of the church, against his wish, and it may be without his notice, gradually recedes. Or if his voice is harsh and his gestures are awkward, if his style is dull and his ideas are thin, the empty pews will speak to him, and now and then there will be wafted to him on a chilling breeze a whisper which will cut. He will become self-conscious in the minor key. This last state is worse than the first. A man conscious of what he has is stronger than a man conscious of what he lacks. Adulation and disparagement are both deadly. Conceit and despondency are twin enemies of pulpit power. Both of them are the children of self-consciousness. A minister is undone whose eyes are fixed on himself. Only by looking away from himself is it possible for him to be saved. Hence in the training of preachers the first glance should be not inward, but outward. Paul, according to an early tradition, began his ministerial career with the question, "Lord, what wilt thou have me to do?" It is because of his critical and immeasurable importance that the preacher in these lectures has been kept in the background. For his own sake his eyes have been turned away from himself. The building of the preacher goes forward during the building of the church.

Certainly no one would claim that the well-being of the preacher is a negligible factor in the complex problem of church building, for here as almost nowhere else, is it incontestably and everlastingly true, "Get your man and all is got." But how to get the man, that is the question. Shall we build him in a vacuum, detached from the world in which he is to work, adding virtue to virtue and grace to grace, until at last, full statured, it is announced to him what he is to do? Or shall we seek him in the church, keeping him under the church ideal, exposing him to church atmospheres and forces, allowing the Christian brotherhood to fashion him after the pattern which the Master gave, and ministering to him through the bonds of fellowship until he becomes a workman of whom no one need be ashamed ?

Humanly speaking, everything depends upon the minister. Music cannot save a church, nor the Bible, nor the sacraments, nor pulpit discourses. Worship dies unless it is kept alive by a living man. Out of the personality of the preacher flow, as Jesus said, the refreshing streams. Most Christian congregations know this. They are caring less and less for scholastic attainments, academic degrees and titles, denominational affiliations, even creedal loyalties — what they want is a man. Things that men pick up in the schools have their value, but they can never take the place of the one thing essential in a preacher — character. Two men go from the same seminary, in the same year, with the same education and the same creed. One succeeds from the beginning, and his successes increase with the seasons. The other fails from the start, and his entire career is a disappointment. It is not a difference in rhetoric, ideas, or training, but a difference in men. They take their texts out of the same Bible, preach the same scheme of doctrinal truth, make use in general of the same ideas and illustrations, but they do not preach the same gospel, for the gospel is truth moulded and vivified by the soul of the man who preaches it. A preacher makes an impression not simply by his words, but by his soul. When words do not penetrate, it is because there is a feeble man behind them. When ideas do not kindle, it is because there is no divine fire in the lips that speak them. Bullets may be of equal size and like material, but the distance to which they travel depends upon the gun. Sermons are bullets. How far they go does not depend upon the text or upon the structure of the sermon, but upon the texture of the manhood of the preacher. The building of the preacher becomes, then, a matter of tremendous moment to every one interested in the building of the church. We cannot afford to run the risk of spoiling him by allowing him to think of himself first.

The reason why no special lecture has been devoted to the building of the sermon is because the subject cannot be treated adequately in a single lecture. All the lectures have been dealing with that interesting and tantalizing theme. Not much has been said about the sermon, but everything has been said in the interest of the sermon. There has been scant attention to the technique of the sermon, but the soul of the sermon has been held steadily in view. There have been no suggestions as to texts, introductions, arguments, climaxes, and perorations, because these things are secondary, and do not reach the root of power in preaching. We have been dealing with things more fundamental. We have faced the aim of preaching, and peered into the things which make preaching worth while. We have considered the kind of atmospheres in which sermons catch fire, and have surveyed the world of thought and feeling from which the streams of pulpit power proceed. Because one says nothing about the letter of the sermon, does he disparage it? God forbid. He exalts it if he uncovers the stupendous work which sermons are to accomplish. All that has been said is designed to help you in the work of preaching. Preaching is your highest business. Nothing can ever take its place. You are to be administrators, but administration will not fill the place of preaching. Unless you are preachers, you are not likely to have much to administer. You are to be organizers, but the organizing gift will never compensate for the lack of the gift of preaching. Men who cannot preach

have ordinarily little to organize. When you see a
man at the head of a large and living church, displaying rare gifts of organization and administration,
do not suppose that these are the gifts by which his
church came into being, or which keep it glad and
strong. He or some one else created it by preaching.
Unless a man knows how to present truth in such a
way as to get it into the blood of those who hear him,
he need never hope for a living, growing, conquering
church, no matter what other gifts he may be
possessed of. Christian people desire of their pastors nothing so much as sermons which will vitalize
and nourish them. They are always shamefaced if
obliged to say, "Our pastor is a good man, but he
cannot preach." Even faithful pastoral service
will not reconcile a congregation to incompetency in
the pulpit. In this the people are not unreasonable.
They have a right to expect and demand that their
pastor shall instruct and comfort and strengthen and
guide them by his sermons. It is the fashion to-day
in certain quarters to speak disparagingly of sermons. One would suppose, from the scornful intonations, that it is almost sacrilegious, if not disreputable,
to go to church for the purpose of listening to a sermon. We are reminded that the purpose of church
attendance is the worship of God, and that sermon

hearing is a modern and secular pastime. All such talk is based on false assumptions. It is assumed that preaching is not worship, and that listening to a sermon is a less religious exercise than that of singing hymns and saying prayers. Both assumptions are without foundation. The true preacher in the act of genuine preaching is worshipping the Almighty, offering to him a sacrifice more costly than any other which it is possible for him to offer in the house of God. If in praise he is loving God with his heart, and in parish work he is loving God with his might, then in the act of preaching he is loving God with his mind, which is also a part of the great commandment. Indeed, in preaching he uses all his heart, and all his soul, and all his mind, and all his strength, as in no other act in all his life. In a sermon the preacher offers himself, soul and body, a living sacrifice unto God. Those who listen to the sermon with docile and attentive hearts, seeking to find God's voice in it, are also engaged in worship. If to worship is to reverence God, and to perform acts of homage and adoration, what higher reverence can be paid him than that offered by a congregation in the act of entering into a fuller apprehension of the meaning of a truth uttered by prophet, or apostle, or God's only Son, and unfolded by a man guided by the Holy

Spirit? The sermon is the climax of public worship. It summons to the throne of God a larger number of faculties than any other act of worship. It calls upon everything within us to bless God's holy name. The pastor of a church is preëminently a preacher. "Feed my sheep," so our Lord said to the leader of the twelve. It is a command which comes to all Christian pastors. "God did not send me to baptize, but to preach the gospel," so said the Master-builder, and let every man remember it, when he is tempted to shirk the arduous duties of a prophet and choose the easier occupations of a priest. The history of the nineteen Christian centuries confirms the wisdom of Paul's great declaration, that it has pleased God to save the world by the foolishness of preaching. Experience shows that when preachers cease to preach, a darkness falls upon the world. There are no golden ages in Christian history, save those made golden by tongues kindled by coals from off God's altar. The preacher holds the keys which unlock the gates of all earth's prisons. The whole world brightens when a man appears able to unfold in syllables of fire the unsearchable riches of Christ. Preaching has had a glorious past. Its future will be more glorious still. The printing-press will never supersede the human tongue. Books will never

drive out the spoken word.   So long as the heart is
human, so long will it respond to a tongue full of
grace and truth.   Never has the world been so rich
in printing-presses as now, and never have the
churches been so clamorous for preachers.   The call
is loud, and it comes from every quarter.   Any man
who knows how to preach is certain of a hearing.
There is no question which the authorities of our
schools of theology ought to ask with greater frequency and earnestness than "How can we better
train our students to become more effective, masterful, triumphant preachers?"   No matter what else
a seminary may do, it does not do the chief thing if
it does not send into the churches well-equipped and
able preachers.

But what is it to preach, and how can one make
himself a preacher?   Here again we are thrown
back on the basal fact, that the sermon depends on
the man.   The sermon is, indeed, the man.   The
man himself must be a sermon.   Preaching is not
an art in the sense in which sculpture, music, and
painting are arts.   It resembles these, but it tran-
scends them all.   The work of the artist can be
divorced from his character.   In preaching it is the
character of the preacher which is the preacher's
power.   Preaching is not a trick which can be

mastered some bright morning, or a secret which can be transmitted from one man to another for a consideration. There is a stupid fellow mentioned in the Book of the Acts, who supposed he could share in the apostles' power by the payment of a sum of money. Stupidity of that sort has not yet vanished from the earth. Even to-day there are men who think that the chief thing in preaching is an artful use of the voice, or a crafty combination of gestures, or a cunning carving of diction, or an expert jugglery of illustrations, or a dexterous manœuvring of ideas, or a clever and impressive display of learning. In this view, preaching is a sort of magic, a sleight of hand or of tongue, an ingenious piece of legerdemain by which souls are mesmerized and the boundaries of God's kingdom extended. The sermon is a contrivance which can be wrought out by an adroit schemer, a strategem which can be laid by a long-headed intriguer, a device which can be created by an industrious artificer. Men who hold this view sometimes go to hear preachers preach in order to learn the secret of their power. They never find out. God hides certain things from the wise and prudent — and also from fools. The man who thinks that preaching is a trick of voice, or thought, or language, never learns how to preach. No men are so wearisome in the pulpit as the men who know they have good voices, and are evidently making an effort to let their hearers know it too. The best thing that a preacher can do with his voice is to hide it. The best voice for preaching is the voice that no one ever hears. Gestures which are striking make an impression the first few times, but if they keep on striking they give pain. Eloquence is good occasionally when it comes by the will of Heaven, but no congregation can endure eloquence every Sunday for five consecutive years. Manufactured eloquence is declamation, and declamation is not eloquence at all. It is a wooden imitation of celestial fire, and is a great weariness. A beautiful style, so beautiful that the rustling of the verbal finery drowns the music of the thought, is also a burden. When all the sentences roll out after the fashion of those of Macaulay or of Burke, men sigh for relief. The best pulpit style is the style that is not seen. Blessed is the preacher who succeeds in beating his style down into invisibility. Voice and language ought to be like the atmosphere, life-supporting but invisible. Illustrations are also a nuisance, unless they grow up naturally like flowers along the path which the sermon takes. Expert illustrators grow irksome after the second year. Quotations are also gewgaws which entertain for a season, and then lose their charm. They never impress any but the unlettered, for all men who are acquainted with the world of books know where and how to get them. Stringing quotations is like stringing beads, it requires no intellect, and is hardly serious business for a full-grown man. It is only when the words of other men force themselves by sheer strength of undeniable superiority into the company of your sentences, and bend themselves whole-heartedly to the task of carrying on your thought, that they can be considered other than impertinent and mischievous interlopers. As for ideas, a preacher can have too many of them. Great thoughts are oppressive if too abundant. It is not thoughts but thought that a congregation wants, and you cannot have thought without a thinker. The ideal preacher is not a retailer of beautiful thoughts, but a man who can bring to the discussion of every moral and spiritual question the illumination of a sane and discriminating mind. Learning is also out of place in the pulpit. Learned sermons are the easiest of all to write, and the most fatiguing to those who hear them. Any one can write a learned sermon who is alone with an encyclopedia for half a dozen hours. Many a church has had its

life crushed out by the learning of its pastor. All
these things — voice, gesture, rhetoric, illustrations,
quotations, ideas, learning — have a certain value,
but they are at best superficialities, and all of
them, unless backed up by something better, soon
grow thin and tame. After a little time artificial
elocution becomes unbearable, rhetorical display
unendurable, excessive illustration insufferable, the
exploitation of novel or abstract ideas intolerable.
Nothing wears but manhood. To remain ten or
twenty years in the same parish, a preacher must be
very simple and very true. Goodness never grows
stale. Love never becomes monotonous. An industrious man in good health with disciplined powers, whose life is hid with Christ in God, can speak
year after year to the same people with the dew of
the morning always on his message. Preaching
is primarily a matter of manhood. The sermon
depends on the mass of the man. His character
must be massive, or he cannot do the work. One
sometimes hears an expression which tells much.
"He is not big enough man for the place." Is
he not educated? Yes. Is he not clever?
Very. Bright? Exceedingly. Brilliant? Often.
And yet not big enough for the place! The
world makes a distinction between a man

and his gifts.   The Church of God must have the man.   The variety and nature of his talents come up for consideration later.   A sermon is not a manufactured product, but a spiritual creation.   It is not a machine which a man can construct in his sermonic shop, and set it running in the pulpit like the electric toys which one sees sometimes on the corner of the city street.   A sermon is an exhalation, a spiritual vapor emerging from the oceanic depths of the preacher's soul.   It is an emanation, an efflux, an effluence flowing from an interior fountain hidden in the depths of personality. It is an efflorescence, an outflowering of beautiful things whose home is in the blood.   It is a perfume from spiritual roses blossoming in the garden of the heart.   It is fruit growing on the tree of a man's life.   "A good tree cannot bring forth evil fruit, neither can a corrupt tree bring forth good fruit." Make the tree good.   A sermon is the life-blood of a Christian spirit.   A preacher dies in the act of preaching.   He lays down his life for his brethren.   He saves others, himself he cannot save.   The pulpit is a Golgotha in which the preacher gives his life for the life of the world.   Preaching is a great work. To do it as God wants it done, the preacher must be a good man, full of the Holy Ghost and of faith.

And now let me speak, not by way of commandment, but by way of counsel; not as presenting a revelation, but only my judgment. It is not good, it seems to me, to resort to various nostrums which have been prepared for the preacher's uses, or to lean too heavily upon sundry mechanical devices which have been created for the purpose of helping the minister on his way. Crutches are good for cripples, and tonics are good for invalids, but young men starting on their work in the ministry ought to walk on their own feet, uncoddled. Books of illustrations are good books — to keep away from. They have no place on the shelves of a man who wants to grow. Let the preacher get his own illustrations. If he has eyes and ears they will come to him in crowds — crying like free children of God : "Here we are, use us." The importance of illustration in the pulpit has been vastly overestimated, and many a preacher has degenerated into a relator of anecdotes and repeater of stale stories. If a man has anything worth illustrating, he will have no difficulty in finding illustrations, but if his chief ambition is to collect images, likenesses, and pictures, he is likely to remain a child in intellect all his life. There is no joy in the ministry, if life is reduced to a haggard hunt after new and striking

illustrations. The preacher who cries out in dis-
may : "Wherewithal shall my sermon be pictorially
clothed?" should read again the exhortation :
"Seek first the Kingdom," with its accompanying
promise that to those who do this, all things needful
will be added. Books of "Great Thoughts" are
also a delusion. No man can entertain ten thousand great thoughts, or even one thousand. They
simply encumber and suffocate the mind. The
thoughts which a congregation needs are not numerous, and if too many are administered at any one
time the mind is surfeited and sinks into a stupor.
The preacher should also beware of note-books,
scrap-books, envelopes for clippings, cases of boxes
and drawers for the storing away of sermonic
material. All such devices have their legitimate
place, but they can easily become a source of peril.
They take a deal of time, and a man may form the
habit of using his scissors when he ought to be using
his head. It is possible to have a hundred huge
envelopes bulging with sermonic treasures, while the
mind is distressingly spindling and lean. It is far
more important to keep the heart full than to have
a lot of things laid away in drawers. Many a man
has hewed out for himself at infinite pains cisterns
which cannot hold the kind of water for which

U

humanity is thirsting.   Facts and figures, statistics
and records, odds and ends of information, — this is
not the material on which souls feed and grow.   A
man should get his sermons not out of a scrap-book
but out of himself.   Like the spider, he should
weave his web out of his own substance.

It is not well to cultivate the homiletic habit, the
habit of demanding a pound of sermonic flesh from
every Antonio you chance to meet.   This habit will
grow upon you in spite of all that you can do, and
may possibly drown you along with thousands of
others in the pool of professionalism.   One ought
not to be thinking shop all the time.   A man who
is always working for sermons is as foolish as the
man who is always working for money.   Both men
may say that they are seeking wealth to be used for
the good of others, but it is not healthful to do one
thing — no matter what it is — all the time.   A
preacher ought to be able to look upon a landscape
without screwing illustrations out of it, or enjoy
a sail upon the Rhine without working the castles
then and there into a course of next winter's sermons, or play with children without squeezing from
them suggestions which may be put to use in the
prayer-meeting.   The homiletic habit is a leech.
It sucks the blood, and leaves the man anæmic.

Landscapes and historic ruins and children, and all other lovely things, are to be enjoyed. They are themselves their own excuse for being, and the preacher should revel in them with no thought of ulterior ends. We wrong a book when we read it simply for things which we can use. It is desecration of a poem to read it for fine phrases with which to deck a sermon, and we wrong the masterpiece of an historian when we follow him only for an illustration with which to brighten up an argument. It is only when we gloriously forget ourselves — as Mrs. Browning has reminded us — and plunge headlong into the depths of the author's thought, that we get out of a book the best thing which the book has to give. In listening to great men speak, the preacher ought to forget that he too is a speaker. He ought not to fix his gaze on the speaker's voice, his gestures, or his adjectives. He ought not to attempt to put into his note-book the things which the speaker says. All that he can get into his note-book is a few fine phrases, a dozen noble sentiments or ideas. But what are these compared with the great things which the hearer might be receiving ! The things most precious are subtle things which cannot be caught on the end of a pencil — disinthralment, enchantment, exaltation, the air of a great height,

While the writer is jotting down a few notions and phrases, he is losing much of the glow of the speaker's soul. It is the flash of the spirit and not the words of the lips which is the best thing which a great man has to give. Catch that and you have an imperishable possession. To feel upon one's life the hot breath of a great heart, to drink into one's being the life of a great soul in one of its great moments, is a privilege which does not come often and which should be valued above rubies and fine gold. We are never the same after we have once entered into the feeling of a man genuinely great, after we have been fused by the fire of his burning spirit. Do not sit aloof as a critic, noting in cold blood trifling incidents of movement and accidents of manner; get near him, go with him, think with him, feel with him, live with him. Let him expand you, exalt you, cleanse you. Go with him. He sees something. He is following a gleam. Try to see what he sees. A gleam which the eye once catches never fades. Phrases fade out of the memory, ideas lose their distinctness of form, but a light that has once shone into the soul becomes a part of the soul's life forever. Do not be a critic whenever you can be something better. A critic even at his best is only a second-rate man. The men of the highest

rank are creators. It is the creators who make
the world. Preachers are called to be creators.
They are to create new atmospheres, new characters, new worlds. They should develop, therefore,
their creative faculties, the imagination and all the
powers by which the soul admires and hopes and
loves. Receptivity, impressionability, spiritual sensitiveness, sympathy, responsiveness, the genius for
merging the soul in the souls of others — these are
the powers which the preacher needs. The critic
always thinks that he goes deep, but he never goes
deep enough to find the secret of life. We cannot
go deep by our critical faculty. The critical faculty
is an anatomist, and an anatomist goes only deep
enough to find bones. With the scalpel one can
reach the skeleton, but never the source and home
of life. You cannot find a speaker's power by dis-
section. You may analyze his arguments, pick to
pieces his phrases, catalogue his pictures, but these
are only bones. You find his life only when your
soul goes out to meet him. Drink at the fountain
of his life, eat his flesh, drink his blood, that you
also may live. What this world needs is not a
fuller knowledge of bones, but a more abundant
measure of vitality.

It is possible to work too long upon a sermon.

The sermon may become an idol, before which the preacher prostrates his powers in worship. This is the temptation that besets men who have the artistic temperament, and who have an eye for delicate shadings and an ear for the finer melodies of speech. Before the preacher is aware of it, he has forgotten his congregation, and is thinking exclusively of the masterpiece which is to be exhibited in the church salon next Sunday morning. This is a sin which, when it is finished, brings forth death. The preacher becomes increasingly fastidious. He is finical in the use of dainty and perfumed words. He paints his picture in such delicate tints that they cannot be seen by persons seated in the back pew. Hypercritical in his taste, he falls into various forms of affectation, and, unless arrested in his downward course, he sinks into the degradation of a rhetorical fop. His sermon is provokingly faultless, unhumanly regular, gloriously null. It is possible to increase as an artist, and at the same time decrease as a preacher. The preacher has lost his power when his sermons, like superb works of art, stand out before his congregation in the marble coldness of finished statues. Work like this impoverishes a preacher. He spends time upon his sermon which ought to be spent upon himself.   The polishing of sentences is a poor way of feeding a man who must preach.   The preacher needs constant supplies of nourishment, and most of his morning hours must be devoted, not to sermon building, but to the building of his soul. The preparation for the specific sermon may be crowded into a few hours, but the preparation of himself should go on all the time.   Young men, ignorant of the laws of soul nutrition, sometimes wear themselves thin in a few years by devoting themselves too exclusively to the work of sermon preparation.   They give themselves no time for that broad and brooding study, extended over many fields, without which the mind deteriorates and ceases to be productive.   In the earlier years, a young preacher must of necessity spend many hours each week upon his sermons, for he is as yet an un-practised worker, and must learn by laborious effort to accumulate material and to give shape and edge to his style.   But every preacher who de-sires to make his pastorate long, must, as rapidly as possible, cut down the hours devoted to sermon writing, in order that he may have more abundant opportunity to work upon himself.   He should aim so to discipline his powers that by and by he shall be able to write a sermon in a single morning.   If a man is industrious and keeps his mind and heart brimful, there is no reason why he should not, after a few years of practice, give shape to his Sunday message between breakfast time and noon. A genius now and then will do it in a single hour.

Let the preacher then work for increased vitality. He can do little unless he is a vital man. His work is to vitalize, and a man cannot give what he himself does not possess. Like the Master, the preacher comes that men may have life, and that they may have it more abundantly. A preacher impoverished in his spirit, diminishes the sum of the spiritual power of the world. He must in all his nature be sensitive and life creating. If he cannot feel a thrill of joy, no one will be thrilled by any glad thing he says. If he cannot suffer an agony, no heart will be pierced by any tone which his voice can utter. A preacher must be intensely human. He must be rich in laughter and in tears. He must be able to rejoice and weep, to entertain those mighty hopes which make men feel they are immortal, and to burn with those flaming enthusiasms which the elect of God in every age have known. The preacher must avoid all courses of life which lower his vitality and cause a shrinkage of the capacities of the heart. Humanity must throb full volumed in him. No man can keep himself alive by saying true and lovely things. He must live and love and suffer. He must purchase with his blood the church for which the Messiah died. He must fill up that which is lacking of the afflictions of Christ.

Only a man full of life dares to be himself. Emaciated men are timid, and men stunted by living exclusively with books dwindle into shadows and echoes. It is when one's life is merged in the life of the race, and the tide of humanity ebbs and floods in one's veins, that one enters into the experiences of a son of the Highest. Every soul is original. There are no duplicates in the world of personality. Every man possesses a combination of traits and talents never before approximated, and never to be repeated. Every preacher is original who dares to be himself. It matters not that he is ordained to preach truths that have been preached already ten thousand times. The words of the New Testament are ancient but not antiquated, its ideas are antique but not archaic, its principles are venerable but not out of date, and the one thing needed to cause the words to burn, the ideas to glow, and the principles to grip, is a preacher who has become a new man in Christ. The oldest commonplaces are no longer trite after they have passed through the red blood of a man redeemed. The preacher who preaches the old doctrines out of his own heart, will find men listening to him as men listened to Paul and Barnabas, and although men have been long familiar with the words, they will go home saying, "We have never heard it after this fashion."

A man who thinks and works and grows is always interesting. The secret of an extended pastorate is a growing man. Young men are sometimes daunted by the fact that all the truths of Christianity are wrinkled and gray-headed. The Christian preacher is ordained for the proclamation of commonplaces. Brotherhood and service, love and forgiveness, hope and mercy, who can make these verbal bones live? Only a living soul can do it. A man half dead cannot do it. A man with a shrivelled heart cannot do it. Only a man in whom Christ dwells richly can give sparkle to the trite, and immortal freshness to things that have lost their bloom. The Old World needs an old gospel. Many things that are new are not true, and all things that are true are not new. The Old World tragedy goes on as from the beginning, and there is no remedy but the one that is old — "Jesus Christ, the same yesterday, to-day, and forever,"

the old, old story of the changeless love of the un-
changing God.   It is a commonplace, but it comes
with the startling flash of a new revelation whenever
spoken by a tongue which throws into it the fresh
joy of an understanding and loving heart. It is
the man that makes the sermon.   The man is the
sermon.   That is why it is impossible to print a
sermon.   No sermon has ever yet been printed.
We print the words, but the words are nothing but
the skeleton, and the spiritual body of the sermon
is the personality of the man.   One cannot account
for Peter's power on the day of Pentecost by reading
the report of Peter's sermon, nor can one account
for the effect produced by any of the kings of
Christian speech by a study of what the reporters
have preserved.   Not what the preacher says but
what he is — this constitutes the sermon.

To preach with the power of Christ one must
have something of the heart of Christ. He is
meek and lowly of heart.   Humility is the queen of
the Christian virtues.   In the list of the Beatitudes
it is Humility to which the first crown is given.
Unless a man becomes as a little child, he cannot
enter the kingdom of heaven, and unless he remains
a little child, he can make no progress therein.
The man who is always teaching must be evermore

the church, let us not forget how the church builds
the preacher. The church is the preacher's school
in which he learns his lessons. The church is the
preacher's hospital, in which the preacher's maladies
are healed. The church is the preacher's battlefield, on which he learns to fight the foes of God and
man. The church is the preacher's home, in which
he gains the Christian virtues and comes into
possession of the Christian graces. It is while he is
knitting the hearts of men together that his own
sympathies are expanded and his own affections are
enriched. In planning for the church he cultivates
his mental faculties : reason, foresight, discrimination, judgment, imagination; and in working out his
plan he develops the graces of the heart: longsuffering, patience, gentleness, goodness, temperance,
and meekness. In sacrificing for the church, he
drinks of the cup of which the Master drank, and
comes at last to bear in his body the marks of the
Lord Jesus. Out of the church, texts and ideas come
for the building of his sermons. Out of the church,
illustrations come, simple and natural and illumi-
nating, after the fashion of the illustrations of Jesus.
The church is the preacher's guardian angel. It
bears him up, and keeps him from dashing his foot
against a stone. The vision of the church checks him

when tempted to enter on downward courses, and braces him in his shadowed hours. Her majesty holds him upright, her dignity makes him strong. The greatness of the privilege of working for her shames him out of cheap ambitions and thrills him with desires to be a nobler man. Through the church Christ reaches his hands, moulding him. Master and servant work together through the laborious and glorious days. The preacher learns to love Christ through the church. The preacher preaches to the church, and the church also preaches to the preacher. It breaks the bread of life to him. It teaches him and admonishes him. It gives him his theology. It inspires him and consoles him. It trains him and it disciplines him. It administers to him the sacraments. It is the servant of the Lord, and it does what the Lord himself cannot now do. Christ exists no longer in the realm of space and time. His home is in the realm of spirit. But his church exists in the temporal and spatial world, and through it he communicates with those who love him. To serve the church is serving him. To love the church is loving him. He accepts this love and service, and through the church there flows back to those who serve and love him the fulness of his grace and benediction.

The church teaches the minister to pray. No